The Deep Wells

Collection

Volume One

H. L. Robertson

No part of this publication may be reproduced, stored in a retrieval system or transmitted in any way by any means, electronic, mechanical, photocopy, recording or otherwise without the prior permission of the author except as provided by USA copyright law.

Scripture quotations marked (kjv) are taken from the *Holy Bible, King James Version*, Cambridge, 1769. Used by permission. All rights reserved.

Book design copyright © 2017 by Fairhaven Media. All rights reserved.
Cover design by H L Robertson
Interior design by H L Robertson

Published in the United States of America

1. Religion / Biblical Criticism & Interpretation / General
2. Religion / Biblical Commentary / General
16.03.31

ISBN: 978-1-94772-900-1

Counsel in the heart of man is like deep water; but a man of understanding will draw it out.
Prov 20:5

4

The Bridegroom Cometh

The Mystery of the Ten Virgins

Introduction

In Matthew chapter 25 Jesus gives his followers what is almost universally known as the "Parable of the Ten Virgins". In this parable we see a mystery begin to unfold. Jesus is at the end of his earthly ministry and is answering his disciples' questions about the end of the world; or the end of the age as some translate it. In chapters 24 and 25 he gives his followers a final series of parables; all relating to his second coming and final judgment. Notice that these are kingdom parables and are thus related to the Jews not the church or the Gentiles. In fact, this parable from the 'Olivet Discourse' is for all practical purposes a commentary on his previous teachings on the bridegroom and bride from John chapter 14. Here he gives us a contrast between the description of the bride in John and the ten virgins in this passage. Notice that John 14 is centered solely on the bridegroom and his bride; and yet, in Matthew 25 there is **no mention** of the bride whatsoever. The coming of the bridegroom is mentioned but not the bride. These verses give us insight into the relationships surrounding the bridegroom, but in some ways only serve to deepen the mystery of the bride vis-à-vis the ten virgins. This has led to a misinterpretation of this parable for centuries by well meaning teachers, preachers and scholars who have tried to force a 'square peg'; the church, into the 'round hole'; i.e. the framework of these verses. This has led to all sorts of spurious doctrines and ideas regarding the relationship of Christ to his brethren the Jews and his followers. This was understandable in the early church because as Paul put it, this was a mystery:

Now to him that is of power to stablish you according to my gospel, and the preaching of Jesus Christ, according to the revelation of the mystery, which was kept secret since the world began, But now is made manifest, and by the scriptures of the prophets, according to the commandment of the everlasting God, made known to all nations for the obedience of faith... Romans 16:25-26

If the fullness of the gospel message and the understanding of the mystery of the Gentile church was so hidden until Paul's ministry, it is quite obvious why this was such a thorny issue in the primitive church. The believers who were Jews had no point of reference for deciphering these passages and the poor Gentile believers were totally reliant on Paul's letters and teachings which would have taken years to be fully circulated throughout the known world. In fact, he tells us in 1 Corinthians chapter 2 that satan himself had no clue how this would play out or he never would have crucified Christ!

Howbeit we speak wisdom among them that are perfect: yet not the wisdom of this world, nor of the princes of this world, that come to nought: But we speak the wisdom of God in a mystery, even the hidden wisdom, which God ordained before the world unto our glory: Which none of the princes of this world knew: for had they known it, they would not have crucified the Lord of glory. But as it is written, Eye hath not seen, nor ear heard, neither have entered into the heart of man, the things which God hath prepared for them that love him. But God hath revealed them unto us by his Spirit: for the Spirit searcheth all things, yea, the deep things of God. 1 Cor 2:7-10

In this small book, I will endeavor to bring clarity to this passage so that the light of truth can be shone on the great treasures contained in these scriptures.

[I] Cease not to give thanks for you, making mention of you in my prayers;
That the God of our Lord Jesus Christ, the Father of glory, may give unto you the spirit of wisdom and revelation in the

knowledge of him: The eyes of your understanding being enlightened; that ye may know what is the hope of his calling, and what the riches of the glory of his inheritance in the saints, And what is the exceeding greatness of his power to us-ward who believe, according to the working of his mighty power... Eph 1:18-19

Chapter One

The first thing to understand about this parable, is who the audience is: these are Jewish believers Jesus was talking to. He is giving Jewish followers Jewish answers to the Jewish questions they had just asked him. As I mentioned in the introduction, this parable has been interpreted for centuries as relating to the Gentile church. This passage and others like it have been Shanghaied into a belief system commonly known as 'replacement theology', which replaces Israel, the Jewish people and more importantly God's covenants with them; with the Gentile church thus interpreting all unfulfilled prophecy about the future relationship of God and his people as pertaining to the church. This can lead to a gross misunderstanding of the meaning and intent of this and other parables; not to mention a form of back-handed anti-Semitism which relegates the Jewish people to being a sort of spiritual footnote in religious history.

The second principle to apply here is a proper placement of the passage in the context of its audience' reception of it. What would this have meant to that audience? How would they have interpreted this parable and its basic story? It is key to the correct understanding of his message to grasp the fact that he is describing this parable lesson in terms of the events leading up to a Jewish wedding ceremony and the traditions surrounding it. The listeners in this case would have immediately picked up on this and would have viewed this teaching through the lens of that database of knowledge. They would have understood the message because they understood fully the premise of how he was presenting it to them.

Then shall the kingdom of heaven be likened unto ten virgins, which took their lamps, and went forth to meet the bridegroom. Matthew 25:1

Once again notice that there is no mention of the bride. We must put this story in its proper framework of Jewish tradition and understanding. We have a revelation of this framework in Paul's letters but it is essential to reconcile the Jewish believers and their place in the framework with the Gentile church and its place:

Even the mystery which hath been hid from ages and from generations, but now is made manifest to his saints: To whom God would make known what is the riches of the glory of this mystery among the Gentiles; which is Christ in you, the hope of glory: Col 1:27

We as Gentile believers know and, by and large, understand this mystery and accept the fact that the church IS the bride of Christ. In fact, Paul shows us this principle in one of the seminal scripture passages regarding Christian husbands and wives and how they relate to one another:

Wives, submit yourselves unto your own husbands, as unto the Lord. For the husband is the head of the wife, even as Christ is the head of the church: and he is the saviour of the body. Therefore as the church is subject unto Christ, so let the wives be to their own husbands in every thing. Husbands, love your wives, even as Christ also loved the church, and gave himself for it; That he might sanctify and cleanse it with the washing of water by the word, That he might present it to himself a glorious church, not having spot, or wrinkle, or any such thing; but that it should be holy and without blemish. So ought men to love their wives as their own bodies. He that loveth his wife loveth himself. For no man ever yet hated his own flesh; but nourisheth and cherisheth it, even as the Lord the church: For we are members of his body, of his flesh, and of his bones. For this cause shall a man leave his father and mother, and shall be joined unto his wife, and they two shall be one flesh. This is a great mystery: but I speak concerning Christ and the church. Eph 5:23-32

We, however, generally speaking, do not have nearly as clear an understanding of how our Jewish bothers and sisters fit into the equation. In fact, I believe the problem is just as profound from the viewpoint of Jewish believers. This I believe accounts for what I perceive as an unnatural separation of the Jewish and Gentile bodies of believers that is so pervasive. A proper, if not necessarily complete, revelation of this parable will go a long way in fostering the attempts currently afoot to break down these artificial barriers.

The first and key point to this revelation is the understanding that the 'ten virgins' as Jesus calls them ARE NOT Gentile Christians and they ARE NOT the church. This more than anything I can relate here is totally essential to our ability to put this teaching in proper context so that we can fit all the pieces of this theological puzzle together. As I describe the Jewish wedding traditions and how they relate to this parable in the following chapters, these puzzle pieces will hopefully begin to fall into place.

Chapter Two

In verses two through four of our parable, we begin to see a division or differentiation within the ten virgins:

And five of them were wise, and five were foolish. They that were foolish took their lamps, and took no oil with them: But the wise took oil in their vessels with their lamps. Matt 25:3-4

We see that five are described as wise and five as foolish. Half have oil in their lamps and half have none. Building on the premise of the last chapter we would say that this cannot possibly apply to the church, as no one would be so cynical as to say that half of the church was unsaved. Some would have us to believe that the five foolish were those who had been saved and had backslidden into reprobation and ultimate destruction in hell.

Again we must look closely at the

premise of the parable and the Jewish wedding ceremony. Specifically the coming of the bridegroom for his espoused bride. This process, and it is a process, is something that every person in Israel would have been closely acquainted with. After all, every married or engaged person had experienced at least part of this. The ten virgins are central to the understanding of Jesus' meaning in this teaching. In the Jewish wedding tradition every young woman who was engaged, or 'espoused' as the scripture puts it, had ten young women - virgins, who were her attendants. There is little doubt that this tradition is the origin of our present day notion of bridesmaids. These ten young women had as their sole responsibility the task of insuring that the bride would be ready for that middle of the night summons by her intended to come out to him and return to his home for the wedding festivities.

After the betrothal ceremony, which

would take place at or near the brides home, the bridegroom would leave the bride behind and return to his home or village. Here he would build a home, or at least a room onto his father's home, for the bride and himself. When **his father** determined that all was in readiness he would then gather his friends and start the journey to his brides home or village. This trip was timed in such a way as to place his arrival at or near midnight. As the party approached her home a trumpet would be blown and a shout raised: 'behold the bridegroom comes, make ready to meet him.' At this point all unmarried women (this would traditionally take place on Tuesday night for virgins and on Wednesday night for widows or divorced women) would arise with their attendants and ready themselves to go see which young woman's groom was approaching. The united party would then return to his village/home and the wedding would be consummated.

In John 14:2-3 we get a glimpse of this tradition through Jesus' teaching concerning the rapture of the church:

In my Father's house are many mansions: if it were not so, I would have told you. I go to prepare a place for you. And if I go and prepare a place for you, I will come again, and receive you unto myself; that where I am, there ye may be also. John 14:2-3

We learn several interesting facts from this scripture. First we see that Jesus describes his return in the rapture in terms of the wedding. Specifically the fact that he is the bridegroom. Second he will return from heaven at an unannounced time. This aligns with and supports the traditional evangelical doctrine of a signless rapture. Next we see that he as the bridegroom is preparing a place in heaven for ourselves as believers and will return via the rapture to receive his bride, the church, to himself. This logically leads us to the 'marriage supper of the lamb' as described in Revelation chapter 19.

But what of those mysterious ten virgins? We must understand **all** the parties involved in the 'process'. First we have the 'friends of the bridegroom' who come with him as seen in John 14. Notice that they are where he is prior to the journey and come with him. Symbolically they represent the Old Testament saints who are in heaven and return with him at the rapture.

John answered and said, A man can receive nothing, except it be given him from heaven. Ye yourselves bear me witness, that I said, I am not the Christ, but that I am sent before him. He that hath the bride is the bridegroom: but the friend of the bridegroom, which standeth and heareth him, rejoiceth greatly because of the bridegroom's voice: this my joy therefore is fulfilled. John 3:28-30

We have already seen that the bride is the church. There then only remains one group unaccounted for: the Jewish nation. We see the ten virgins **at the bride's dwelling**. These are people who are living on the earth during the time of the bridegroom's absence (i.e. the 'church age'). Notice that half go with him in the rapture and half are left. This clearly points to the fact that part of the Jews will be saved and go in the rapture and part will be left in unbelief to endure the tribulation. These Jews that are taken in the rapture are the 'wedding guests' as described in Matthew chapter 22. Many of the ones invited would not come (the unbelieving Jews) and the wayward strangers (the Gentiles) were invited in their place.

The kingdom of heaven is like unto a certain king, which made a marriage for his son, And sent forth his servants to call them that were bidden to the wedding: and they would not come. Again, he sent forth other servants, saying, Tell them which are bidden, Behold, I have prepared my dinner: my oxen and my fatlings are killed, and all things are ready: come unto the marriage. But they made light of it, and went their ways, one to his farm, another to his merchandise: And the remnant took his servants, and entreated them spitefully, and slew them. But when the king heard thereof, he was wroth: and he sent forth his armies, and destroyed those murderers, and burned up their city. Then saith he to his servants, The wedding is ready, but they which were bidden were not worthy. Go ye therefore into the highways, and as many as ye shall find, bid to the marriage. So those servants went out into the highways, and gathered together all as many as they found, both bad and good: and the wedding was furnished with guests. Matt 22:3-10

Now that we have the basic framework of understanding the premise of the parable, let's look deeper into its details.

Chapter Three

In Matthew 24, immediately after the Lord's supper we see the disciples ask Jesus about his coming and the end of the world:

And as he sat upon the mount of Olives, the disciples came unto him privately, saying, Tell us, when shall these things be? and what shall be the sign of thy coming, and of the end of the world? Matthew 24:3

He then begins to teach them concerning these questions, culminating in a discourse on the rapture, tribulation, and second coming. They still apparently fail to grasp the fact that he will be crucified and eventually be taken from them. In fact they didn't really understand the whole scenario until after the resurrection:

When therefore he was risen from the dead, his disciples remembered that he had said this unto them; and they believed the scripture, and the word which Jesus had said. John 2:21

He then proceeds to give them the series of kingdom parables, including that of the ten virgins. Based on the Jewish wedding traditions it should have been obvious that the coming of the bridegroom was to be at an unknown time. He has just told them in the preceding discussion concerning his return:

But of that day and hour knoweth no man, no, not the angels of heaven, but my Father only. Matthew 24:36

As we saw in the last chapter, the ten virgins were supposed to help the bride to remain in a constant state of readiness. The sad truth is that verse five of our text shows that **ALL** the virgins were asleep.

While the bridegroom tarried, they all

slumbered and slept. Matthew 25:5

This is an indictment of the people who are represented by the virgins; namely the Jews. Notice that those who were 'wise' are found to be in the same outward condition as the 'foolish'. All were asleep. It is ironic that in Matthew chapter 26 we see Jesus go into the garden (awaiting the coming betrayal) and telling his disciples to 'watch with me', he goes a little way apart to pray. He comes three separate time to check on them and finds them asleep all three times. After the third time he says:

Sleep on now, and take your rest: behold, the hour is at hand, and the Son of man is betrayed into the hands of sinners. v45

His closest friends and followers were guilty of exactly the sin he had predicted in our text! This failing is not confined to the Jewish people; both Jewish and Gentile followers are strongly warned concerning this by the Apostle Paul in 1 Thessalonians chapter 5:

But of the times and the seasons, brethren, ye have no need that I write unto you. For yourselves know perfectly that the day of the Lord so cometh as a thief in the night. For when they shall say, Peace and safety; then sudden destruction cometh upon them, as travail upon a woman with child; and they shall not escape. But ye, brethren, are not in darkness, that that day should overtake you as a thief. Ye are all the children of light, and the children of the day: we are not of the night, nor of darkness. Therefore let us not sleep, as do others; but let us watch and be sober.
1 Thessalonians 5:2-6

Notice the eerie similarities to the teachings in Matthew chapters 24 and 25. Once again the concept of a sudden and unexpected coming of the bridegroom is brought to focus with the picture of a 'thief in the night'. We are told that we should 'not sleep as do others', and he ends with an admonition that is a striking parallel to Jesus command to his disciples in the garden to 'watch with me'.

While we await his coming we are to know the signs of his coming and await him in vigilance and readiness of heart and mind.

Chapter Four

In our text we see that when the cry came that the bridegroom was coming, the lamps of half of the virgins were ready and the other half were not.

Then all those virgins arose, and trimmed their lamps. And the foolish said unto the wise, Give us of your oil; for our lamps are gone out. But the wise answered, saying, Not so; lest there be not enough for us and you: but go ye rather to them that sell, and buy for yourselves. Matt 25:7-9

An important point to recognize is that the lamps weren't 'gone out' as KJV renders it, but this phrase is in the Greek tense known as an historical present. A much better rendering would be 'our lamps are **going out**'. The fact was that as Jesus spoke these words the lamp of the Jewish nation was literally going out. In fact, rabbinical tradition tells us that after the crucifixion, the center 'servant branch' of the temple menorah, which was a representation of Messiah, went out and could never be kept lit again. Thus the prophetic words of Jesus were quite literally fulfilled. Jesus has previously told the people, including the Pharisees, that he was their light:

Then spake Jesus again unto them, saying, I am the light of the world: he that followeth me shall not walk in darkness, but shall have the light of life. John 8:12

Then Jesus said unto them, Yet a little while is the light with you. Walk while ye have the light, lest darkness come upon you: for he that walketh in darkness knoweth not whither he goeth. While ye have light, believe in the light, that ye may be the children of light. These things spake Jesus, and departed, and did hide himself from them. John 12:35-36

The fact that he was rejected by his own

people and their spiritual leaders brought not only darkness, but spiritual blindness upon the whole nation of Israel:

Therefore speak I to them in parables: because they seeing see not; and hearing they hear not, neither do they understand. And in them is fulfilled the prophecy of Esaias, which saith, By hearing ye shall hear, and shall not understand; and seeing ye shall see, and shall not perceive: For this people's heart is waxed gross, and their ears are dull of hearing, and their eyes they have closed; lest at any time they should see with their eyes, and hear with their ears, and should understand with their heart, and should be converted, and I should heal them. Matt 13:14-15

Here Jesus quotes a prophecy from Isaiah concerning this very principle. In Romans, Paul reiterates this idea:

For I would not, brethren, that ye should

be ignorant of this mystery, lest ye should be wise in your own conceits; that blindness in part is happened to Israel, until the fulness of the Gentiles be come in. Romans 11:25

To this day the spiritual blindness that Jesus and Paul spoke of is still pervasive among the Jewish people. Sadly the vast majority are still unprepared for the coming of their Messiah and have 'no oil in their lamps'.

Chapter Five

The text of our parable shows us the arrival of the bridegroom (Christ) for his bride:

And at midnight there was a cry made, Behold, the bridegroom cometh; go ye out to meet him. ... And while they went to buy, the bridegroom came; and they that were ready went in with him to the marriage: and the door was shut.
Matthew 25:6,10

The key point to notice here is that although all were asleep and failed to be fully ready for his coming; in the final event, half were prepared to meet him and went with him to the prepared place he spoke of in John chapter 14. (see chapter 2) This speaks to the fact that a significant portion; some believe literally half, of the Jewish nation will be saved before the rapture occurs. In truth, Jewish people are being evangelized and being saved at a rate that is unprecedented since the time of the early church.

As we saw in chapter 2, the bridegroom would approach the bride's home near midnight ('as a thief in the night') a trumpet would sound and the call for the bride to meet her bridegroom would be made. We see this picture in Paul's first letter to the church at Thessalonica:

For the Lord himself shall descend from heaven with a shout, with the voice of the archangel, and with the trump of God: and the dead in Christ shall rise first: Then we which are alive and remain shall be caught up together with them in the clouds, to meet the Lord in the air: and so shall we ever be with the Lord.
1 Thessalonians 4:17

Notice the trumpet and cry calling forth his bride. This same idea is repeated in Revelation chapter four in John's catching up to heaven in a symbolic picture of the rapture:

After this I looked, and, behold, a door was opened in heaven: and the first voice which I heard was as it were of a trumpet talking with me; which said, Come up hither, and I will shew thee things which must be hereafter. Revelation 4:1

Note that John is a Jewish believer. This verse as well as the parable (and the wedding traditions) show that the wise virgins; i.e. the Jewish believers, will be caught up in the rapture along with the bride and the 'friends of the bridegroom'.

Chapter Six

The tragedy of this scenario is that a huge portion of God's chosen people will miss the rapture and thereby the marriage supper of the lamb. How devastating it will be for those of Jesus' own kindred to realize too late that their Messiah has come and they have been left behind in the clutches of an evil imposter. It is noteworthy to know that the Greek word 'antichristo' does not mean 'against Christ' as our meaning of the prefix anti- would seem to indicate; but rather it means a false Christ. He is a fake and a charlatan who will deceive the huge majority of the world. The Jews who are saved during the tribulation period and flee to the wilderness (most scholars believe Petra is the location) will initially have been taken in but will awaken and flee for their very lives according to Revelation chapter 12:

And there appeared a great wonder in heaven; a woman clothed with the sun, and the moon under her feet, and upon her head a crown of twelve stars: And she being with child cried, travailing in birth, and pained to be delivered. And there appeared another wonder in heaven; and behold a great red dragon, having seven heads and ten horns, and seven crowns upon his heads. And his tail drew the third part of the stars of heaven, and did cast them to the earth: and the dragon stood before the woman which was ready to be delivered, for to devour her child as soon as it was born. And she brought forth a man child, who was to rule all nations with a rod of iron: and her child was caught up unto God, and to his throne. And the woman fled into the wilderness, where she hath a place prepared of God, that they should feed her there a thousand two hundred and threescore days. Rev 12:2-6

Our text shows the despair of those left out of the wedding festivities:

Afterward came also the other virgins,

saying, Lord, Lord, open to us. But he answered and said, Verily I say unto you, I know you not. Watch therefore, for ye know neither the day nor the hour wherein the Son of man cometh. Matt 25:12-13

Here we see that they are simply told 'I know you not'. They are not believers and are left on the outside looking in. I believe this in part corresponds to Zechariah's prophecy:

And I will pour upon the house of David, and upon the inhabitants of Jerusalem, the spirit of grace and of supplications: and they shall look upon me whom they have pierced, and they shall mourn for him, as one mourneth for his only son, and shall be in bitterness for him, as one that is in bitterness for his firstborn. Zechariah 12:10

Notice also in the text that there are **five** wise and **five** foolish virgins. Five is the biblical number for grace. Those who are saved find grace, but those who are left behind will also find grace as indicated in Zechariah's prophecy. The 'spirit of grace' that is poured out will spark a great return of Jewish people's hearts to God. Most end-time prophecy scholars interpret this to indicate a mass revival among God's chosen people resulting in a national or at least massive salvation movement among them. Then the prophecy of blindness and darkness that Jesus proclaimed (see chapter 4) will be reversed:

Strengthen ye the weak hands, and confirm the feeble knees. Say to them that are of a fearful heart, Be strong, fear not: behold, your God will come with vengeance, even God with a recompence; he will come and save you. Then the eyes of the blind shall be opened, and the ears of the deaf shall be unstopped. Then shall the lame man leap as an hart, and the tongue of the dumb sing: for in the wilderness shall waters break out, and streams in the desert. Isaiah 35:4-6

The grace of God that is poured out will produce the fruit of righteousness that God had so long been looking for on his 'fig tree' as described in Luke chapter 13. This will result in the fulfilling of Paul proclamation in Romans 11:26-27:

And so all Israel shall be saved: as it is written, There shall come out of Sion the Deliverer, and shall turn away ungodliness from Jacob: For this is my covenant unto them, when I shall take away their sins. Romans 11:26-27

Conclusion

This parable give us an invaluable insight into the interrelationships of the church, the Jewish believers, the Jewish non-believers, and the bridegroom, Christ himself. By thoroughly and systematically dissecting this passage I believe we come to a place of much greater understanding of how all the puzzle pieces fit and what their roles are. Understanding the basic premise of the parable that the ten virgins represent the Jewish nation both individually and corporately is essential to locating this parable in its proper place in the framework of scriptural knowledge.

Three Covenant Trees

Introduction

Some time ago I began a study of the trees mentioned in scripture. This seemingly pedestrian undertaking has led me on a journey through both the Old and New Testaments. The path has been winding and, at times obscure, but the end result has been a trip well worth taking. I have had true moments of inspiration and revelation that have made this both a challenging and a fulfilling trip; sprinkled with moments of pure joy. The symbolism is deep and rich, and is apparently inexhaustible. There always seemed to be one more 'ah-ah' moment just around the bend.

The jumping off point for this book was the realization early on that the symbolic picture painted by the imagery of these trees was not only profound but interconnected by one central theme. The covenant relationship of God with man, specifically with the Jewish patriarchs and their descendants, was woven throughout the Bible. This unifying theme began to show itself to me much as a jigsaw puzzle starts to reveal itself as you first outline the borders and then slowly, painstakingly fill in the interior. As I began to explore the subject of covenant in relation to the trees, each one told its story. First the fig tree and its national symbolism, then the acacia and its connection to hardship and suffering, and finally the almond, the most obscure of the three and yet possibly the most meaningful.

As you read this book, I sincerely hope you gain as much pleasure and insight from it as I did in researching and writing it.

Hubert Robertson
Lynchburg, Tennessee
July 12, 2014

The Spirit of the Lord GOD is upon me; because the LORD hath anointed me to preach good tidings unto the meek; he hath sent me to bind up the brokenhearted, to proclaim liberty to the captives, and the opening of the prison to them that are bound; To proclaim the acceptable year of the LORD, and the day of vengeance of our God; to comfort all that mourn; To appoint unto them that mourn in Zion, to give unto them beauty for ashes, the oil of joy for mourning, the garment of praise for the spirit of heaviness; that they might be called trees of righteousness, the planting of the LORD, that he might be glorified. Isaiah 61:1-3

Chapter One - Restoration

The fig tree is probably the best known and most scripturally visible of the three trees. It has for the last couple of generations been expounded as the symbol of the nation of Israel; especially among teachers of end-time prophecy and related subjects. It is, in fact, the first botanical species mentioned by name in scripture. Genesis 3:7 tells us that Adam and Eve sewed fig leaves together in a futile attempt to hide their nakedness from God following the fall. This was a type and shadow of what the nation of Israel would later do in trying to cover their rebellion and idolatry:

But Israel, which followed after the law of righteousness, hath not attained to the law of righteousness. Wherefore? Because they sought it not by faith, but as it were by the works of the law. Romans 9:31-32

In the great love poem commonly called Song of Solomon, God describes Israel in romantic terms depicting the glory of spring and the reawakening of life; an allegorical picture of the resurrection:

My beloved spake, and said unto me, Rise up, my love, my fair one, and come away. For, lo, the winter is past, the rain is over and gone The flowers appear on the earth; the singing of birds is come, and the voice of the turtle is heard in our land; The fig tree putteth forth her green figs, and the vines with the tender grape give a good smell. Arise, my love, my fair one, and come away. Song of Solomon 2:10-13

Here we see one of the earliest presentations of the joining of all peoples; the nation of Israel depicted by the fig tree and the Gentile nations depicted by the vineyard. This symbolism is carried on throughout the Old and New Testaments, most notably Paul's discourse in Ephesians chapters two through four about the 'one new man' and 'putting on the new man' showing us that the bride of Christ will be a blended body of both Jewish and Gentile believers.

We will see, however in the ensuing chapters of Song of Solomon that all was not well in the relationship; there was a period of estrangement and separation that followed the initial period of romance and infatuation. This prophetic picture played out between God and Israel as they turned from His true worship to idolatry, following after the gods of the indigenous Canaanite nations as well as, eventually, all the other surrounding cultures.

I found Israel like grapes in the wilderness; I saw your fathers as the firstripe in the fig tree at her first time: but they went to Baalpeor, and separated themselves unto that shame; and their abominations were according as they loved. Hosea 9:10

From the time of the judges to the dispersion of the nation into, first the Assyrian, and then the Babylonian, empires; God repeatedly pleaded with the Israelites to turn from their rebellion and called them to repentance; but the self-destructive pattern continued in a down spiral. Unfortunately, Israel continued to rebel against God, ultimately bringing judgment and destruction to the nation.

And the LORD said, I will remove Judah also out of my sight, as I have removed Israel, and will cast off this city Jerusalem which I have chosen, and the house of which I said, My name shall be there. 2 Kings 23:27

This first embodiment of national Israel came to an end in the successive, crushing conquests of the northern kingdom of Israel by the Assyrians in 722 BC; followed by the southern kingdom of Judah by the Babylonians in 586 BC. In his mercy God eventually brought them out of exile and restored them to their land.

Chapter Two

By the time of Christ, Israel had become 'Judea', a mere remnant of the once great nation God had chosen to bless. They no longer worshipped pagan gods, but they were steeped in idolatry nonetheless. They now worshipped at a most insidious and deceptive altar; that of their own self-righteousness and religious tradition. In Matthew chapter 21 we see Jesus as he rides into Jerusalem in his 'triumphal entry'. He is hailed as the 'Son of David' by many in the crowd. He goes into the temple, greeted by thronging crowds; including many small children, officially offering himself to them as their Messiah. However, when he drives out the merchants and money changers, the Jewish religious leaders rejected him. Their response is to demand to know by what authority he does these things in stopping the temple trade; which was, not incidentally, a source of a significant portion of their wealth. He then leaves

Jerusalem to go to Bethany; probably to Lazarus' home. The next morning as he is returning to Jerusalem, we see the following scene unfold:

Now in the morning as he returned into the city, he hungered. And when he saw a fig tree in the way, he came to it, and found nothing thereon, but leaves only, and said unto it, Let no fruit grow on thee henceforward for ever. And presently the fig tree withered away. Matthew 21:17-19

Here we see an object lesson in a physical manifestation of what has just transpired in the spiritual realm. The fig tree once again represents Israel and the fact that they were not bearing the fruit of righteousness he came seeking from them. Just as Israel had rejected him, he was pronouncing a curse and judgment upon them. In the same way that Israel had been religiously and morally bankrupt for so many centuries during the time of the judges and the kings, they were still spiritually barren. God, who had sent them into exile to break the stronghold of idolatry; then had in his mercy restored them, now foretells their future destruction in this miraculous display of judgment. The fig tree, representing Israel, is shown to be barren and was going to remain so for the duration of this second embodiment of their national life.

During Jesus' 'Olivet Discourse' in Matthew chapters 24 and 25, he gives the disciples further insight into the future of the nation of Israel.

And Jesus went out, and departed from the temple: and his disciples came to him for to shew him the buildings of the temple. And Jesus said unto them, See ye not all these things? verily I say unto you, There shall not be left here one stone upon another, that shall not be thrown down. Matthew 24:1-2

Here we see the foretelling of the

destruction of Jerusalem, and by inference the nation of Israel, by their Roman rulers. The spirit of rebellion toward authority that caused their political and spiritual leaders to rebel against God and to reject Christ, led them to mutiny against Rome. This culminated in the razing of Jerusalem in 70 AD by Titus (who was later to become Caesar in 79 AD) and his army; including the Tenth Legion, who would remain as a military garrison in the remains of Jerusalem.

What came after is an almost complete purging of the land of Jewish people in a second great dispersion. The fig tree had truly withered as Matthew 21 predicted.

Chapter Three

Despite all this judgment and destruction, which left the land of Israel a virtual desolation; there is a third embodiment of national Israel predicted by scripture. Once again these predictions come in the form of symbolic passages relating to the fig tree. The land of Israel, by the end of the nineteenth century was almost deserted. Historical sources say that less than 50,000 people inhabited it. Vast regions along the coast were nothing more than malarial salt swamps. The interior was little better. Centuries of neglect (and intentional destruction, including the Romans sowing the land with salt to inhibit future agriculture) had taken their toll. Anyone who held a literal biblical view of prophetic scriptures predicting the rise of Israel once again as a nation was ridiculed and scoffed at. It was assumed by most that this piece of real estate would remain perpetually in a near desert condition.

In spite of all this, Jesus gives us a hint in Luke chapter 13 that this is not to be the final end of Israel; and that there will be another resurrection of his chosen nation.

He spake also this parable; A certain man had a fig tree planted in his vineyard; and he came and sought fruit thereon, and found none. Then said he unto the dresser of his vineyard, Behold, these three years I come seeking fruit on this fig tree, and find none: cut it down; why cumbereth it the ground? And he answering said unto him, Lord, let it alone this year also, till I shall dig about it, and dung it: And if it bear fruit, well: and if not, then after that thou shalt cut it down. Luke 13:6-9

The prevailing wisdom among many Christians became the idea that national Israel would never exist again as a literal entity and that 'spiritual Israel', i.e. the church had replaced the physical one. This destructive doctrine tends to lead to a feeling of superiority and arrogance in the church and, in many cases, to a form of insidious, backhanded anti-Semitism. Nothing could be further from God's truth or his intentions. The very people who should be cheering for Israel's restoration, actually have often times hindered it, by refusing to acknowledge that the land was theirs and could or should be returned to the Jewish people.

The Lord had other plans for his chosen land. Jesus in the Olivet discourse, after giving his disciples an overview of prophetic history, presents them with the following benchmark on the prophetic calendar:

Now learn a parable of the fig tree; When his branch is yet tender, and putteth forth leaves, ye know that summer is nigh: So likewise ye, when ye shall see all these things, know that it is near, even at the doors. Verily I say unto you, This generation shall not pass, till all these things be fulfilled. Matthew 24:33-34

We see from this passage that once again, God in his infinite mercy and grace was going to restore Israel to their land and rebuild the nation. The fig tree is once again in full bloom: the land is now a fruitful garden above and beyond anything the world could have imagined. Also notice that the scripture says "When his branch is tender". The Hebrew noun for fig tree is feminine in gender and yet the pronoun is 'his'. This confirms and stresses the fact that this is referring to Israel (Jacob) and his offspring in their covenant relationship to God.

Chapter Four - Redemption

The acacia tree is far less well known than the fig tree. Part of this is because it, its wood, and its thorns are mentioned by several names and in various contexts that don't necessarily lend themselves to the recognition of the type of tree from which the thorns and wood derive. The first mention of the acacia, called 'Shittim wood' in the King James translation, is in Exodus chapter twenty-five:

And the LORD spake unto Moses, saying, Speak unto the children of Israel, that they bring me an offering: of every man that giveth it willingly with his heart ye shall take my offering. And this is the offering which ye shall take of them; gold, and silver, and brass, And blue, and purple, and scarlet, and fine linen, and goats' hair, And rams' skins dyed red, and badgers' skins, and shittim wood, Oil for the light, spices for anointing oil, and for sweet incense,

Onyx stones, and stones to be set in the ephod, and in the breastplate. And let them make me a sanctuary; that I may dwell among them. According to all that I shew thee, after the pattern of the tabernacle, and the pattern of all the instruments thereof, even so shall ye make it. Exodus 25:1-9

Here we see that acacia wood was one of the primary building block materials from which the tabernacle was to be constructed. The acacia tree is plentiful in most all areas of the Middle East in one of its forms or another. This in contrast to the other items in the Exodus 25 'shopping list', which were all valuable to some degree; some of them prohibitively so. Yet, the children of Israel brought materials in such abundance that they were eventually told to stop bringing offerings. The very act of harvesting this plentiful wood, however, is a painful prospect. The trees are one large mass of thorns; reaching the heart of the tree to cut the wood with bronze age tools would be a daunting task to say the least. Here we reach the symbolic basis for the use of this particular wood; the idea that the redemption that was symbolized by it would only be achieved through suffering.

In Genesis chapter three God pronounces His curses on mankind and consequently on the earth for man's sin and rebellion:

And unto Adam he said, Because thou hast hearkened unto the voice of thy wife, and hast eaten of the tree, of which I commanded thee, saying, Thou shalt not eat of it: cursed is the ground for thy sake; in sorrow shalt thou eat of it all the days of thy life; Thorns also and thistles shall it bring forth to thee; and thou shalt eat the herb of the field; In the sweat of thy face shalt thou eat bread, till thou return unto the ground; for out of it wast thou taken: for dust thou art, and unto dust shalt thou return. Genesis 3:18-19

Here, we catch a glimpse of God's plan for redemption. In verses 14 and 15 God had already warned Satan of the coming 'seed of the woman' that would bruise (crush) his head. This was the very first Messianic prophecy. He then goes on in the verses above to pronounce what seems to be a devastating curse: for the ground to bring forth thorns and thistles. Yet, in the curse there is also the cure! The very thorns of the curse are used time and again as a symbol and/or an agent of God's redemptive plan.

Chapter Five-The Abraham Connection

In the sacrifice of Isaac by his father Abraham we see a beautiful and panoramic view of God's master plan of redemption. Abraham is told by God to offer Isaac; his son of covenant promise as a burnt offering to the Lord, 'upon one of the mountains which I will tell thee of.' (Genesis 22:2) Rabbinical commentaries say that Abraham knew which mountain God intended because the 'Shekinah glory' rested there. Abraham obeys and begins the journey to Mount Moriah; what is now known as the temple mount in Jerusalem. He does this despite the promise by God to make a great nation of Isaac's descendants. Abraham proceeds to tell his servants 'Abide ye here with the ass; and I and the lad will go yonder and worship, and come again to you.' (Genesis 22:5) So complete was his faith that he believed God would raise Isaac up if he obeyed and sacrificed him.

By faith Abraham, when he was tried, offered up Isaac: and he that had received the promises offered up his only begotten son, Of whom it was said, That in Isaac shall thy seed be called: Accounting that God was able to raise him up, even from the dead; Hebrews 11:18-19

He then tells the questioning Isaac that 'God will provide Himself a lamb'. This story reaches its climax with Abraham prepared to slay Isaac only to be stopped by an angel. He then sees God's provision:

And Abraham lifted up his eyes, and looked, and behold behind him a ram caught in a thicket by his horns: and Abraham went and took the ram, and offered him up for a burnt offering in the stead of his son. Genesis 22:13

The word for thicket is 'cebak' from the Hebrew root for 'entangled'. The same root is used in Nahum 1:10 'folden together as thorns'. The cursed thorn shows up as an agent of God's redemptive plan. Abraham who was in covenant with God had offered his son of covenant to God and by ancient covenant law God was obligated to return the gesture with a gift of equal or greater value. The ram in the thicket was a temporary substitutionary sacrifice, but the permanent substitute was embodied in the person of God's Son, Jesus Christ. The ram which was caught by his horns, a symbol of his strength, was no doubt able to by his strength rip himself free from the thorns; yet he was held, not by the power of the thorns, but by the will of a sovereign God. By the same token, Jesus who had emptied himself of His divine power and 'humbled himself, and became obedient unto death, even the death of the cross' was held to that cross by the will of His Father:

And he went a little further, and fell on his face, and prayed, saying, O my

Father, if it be possible, let this cup pass from me: nevertheless not as I will, but as thou wilt. Matthew 26:39

Chapter Six–The Tabernacle & the Cross

As Abraham's offspring multiplied and the nation of Israel was born the thread of the acacia continued. In the Tabernacle of Moses we see it entwined in the design of the Tabernacle furniture; each piece full of symbolic meaning and foreshadowing of Christ's coming. The great altar, altar of incense, and the ark of the covenant were all constructed of acacia wood overlaid with pure gold.

Space would fail me to cover all that ground here, but let's look at the ark in particular. Exodus 25:10-22 describes it in great detail:

And they shall make an ark of shittim wood: And thou shalt overlay it with pure gold, within and without shalt thou overlay it, and shalt make upon it a crown of gold round about. And thou shalt put into the ark the testimony which I shall give thee. And thou shalt make a mercy seat of pure gold: two cubits and a half shall be the length thereof, and a cubit and a half the breadth thereof. And thou shalt put the mercy seat above upon the ark; and in the ark thou shalt put the testimony that I shall give thee. And there I will meet with thee, and I will commune with thee from above the mercy seat, from between the two cherubims which are upon the ark of the testimony Exodus 25:11-22(excerpts)

The fact that it was built of wood and covered with pure gold represents the fact that our fallen cursed nature and the works of our hands (the wooden structure) were totally inadequate before the Lord. The golden covering points to fact that God's righteousness, through Christ is imputed to us to cover and sanctify us. The mercy seat was the place that the high priest poured out the sin offering once a year on the day of atonement for a covering for Israel's sins for that year.

When Christ died on the cross He was wearing a crown of thorns; no doubt from the acacia tree (the Greek 'acanthus' is the direct equivalent to the Hebrew 'qowts' for thorns) Again we see the thread of redemption running through the acacia's covenant symbolism. His blood was shed for our sins and was our atonement:

Being justified freely by his grace through the redemption that is in Christ Jesus: Whom God hath set forth to be a propitiation through faith in his blood, to declare his righteousness for the remission of sins Romans 3:24-25

Notice the word 'propitiation' (atonement). This is the Greek word 'hilasterion'. It is the word for the mercy seat! In fact, it is the word that the Greek Septuagint translation of the Old Testament uses in Exodus 25 for the mercy seat. Apparently God considers the atonement and the place of atonement to be synonymous. Not only did Christ die as our atonement and redeem us from the curse of sin, but he did it while wearing the very symbol of the curse that His Father had pronounced on mankind in Genesis chapter three. This sacrifice was foreseen by Abraham in a vision:

Then said the Jews unto him, Now we know that thou hast a devil. Abraham is dead, and the prophets; and thou sayest, If a man keep my saying, he shall never taste of death. Art thou greater than our father Abraham, which is dead? and the prophets are dead: whom makest thou thyself ... (Jesus said) Your father Abraham rejoiced to see my day: and he saw it, and was glad. Then said the Jews unto him, Thou art not yet fifty years old, and hast thou seen Abraham? Jesus said unto them, Verily, verily, I say unto you, Before Abraham was, I am. John 8:53-58

In Genesis we see a clue to this vision that often goes overlooked:

And Abraham called the name of that place Jehovahjireh: as it is said to this day, In the mount of the LORD it shall be seen. Genesis 22:14

Chapter Seven - Resurrection

The third covenant tree is the almond. Long considered a harbinger of spring and new life by Israel and its neighbors; the almond, native to this region, is budding in January when all other trees are still in their winter dormant stage. Thus, it has for millennia had a strong place in Hebrew tradition and rabbinical commentaries as a sign of resurrection. It is also considered to be a sign of watchfulness and promise due to its early flowering.

In Numbers 17 we see God use the sign of a dead rod budding as a sign that He had chosen the tribe of Levi to be the priests and leaders of the nation of Israel.

And it shall come to pass, that the man's rod, ...shall blossom. And it came to pass, that on the morrow Moses went into the tabernacle of witness; and, behold, the rod of Aaron for the house of

Levi was budded, and brought forth buds, and bloomed blossoms, and yielded almonds. Num 17:5-8 excerpts

This budded rod was placed in the ark of the covenant as a sign to any that murmured against God's appointed leaders. Rabbinical tradition says that the rod bore sweet almonds on one side and bitter almonds on the other. If Israel followed God and were obedient the sweet almond side would bear However, if they were disobedient and rebellious the bitter side would bear almonds. By this sign the high priest could always tell the prevailing spiritual condition of the nation.

This rod was a symbol of Christ as the Messiah: he was the rod with branches both good and bad shooting off. (In John's gospel He describes himself as 'the true vine' and goes on to describe the unfruitful branches.) The symbol of the rod is carried on in chapter three of Zechariah's prophecy:

Hear now, O Joshua the high priest, thou, and thy fellows that sit before thee: for they are men wondered at: for, behold, I will bring forth my servant the BRANCH. And speak unto him, saying, Thus speaketh the LORD of hosts, saying, Behold the man whose name is The BRANCH; and he shall grow up out of his place, and he shall build the temple of the LORD:...Zechariah 3:8; 6:12

Christ is 'the Branch' and will divide the sheep (believers) from the goats (unbelievers) as we see in the Olivet discourse:

...as a shepherd divideth his sheep from the goats: And he shall set the sheep on his right hand, but the goats on the left. Matthew 25:32-33

Similarly, the rod had both sweet and bitter almonds on it and thus we have His admonition from Matthew chapter seven: "Ye shall know them by their fruits."

The almond found its way into the tabernacle as well. The menorah or lampstand in the Holy place was decorated with ornaments in the shape of almond blossoms.

And thou shalt make a candlestick of pure gold: of beaten work shall the candlestick be made: his shaft, and his branches, his bowls, his knops, and his flowers, shall be of the same.   And six branches shall come out of the sides of it; three branches of the candlestick out of the one side, and three branches of the candlestick out of the other side: Three bowls made like unto almonds, with a knop and a flower in one branch; and three bowls made like almonds in the other branch, with a knop and a flower: so in the six branches that come out of the candlestick. Exodus 25:32-33

The center shaft/lamp is called the

'servant branch' and is representative of Messiah. Six is the number of man; thus the six branches represent mankind. The fact that there are three on each side represents God's love for all man; both those who are righteous and those who are unrighteous. All will judged and parted right and left.

Chapter Eight-The Firstfruits

We have examined the Old Testament symbolism in the almond tree; now let's look at the hidden meanings in relation to Jesus as Saviour and Messiah. Aaron's rod that budded was such a profound sign that it was preserved in the ark of the covenant. By the same token, Jesus' resurrection was the seminal event of not only His ministry but, in fact, of all human history. Jesus himself used His resurrection as the sole sign that would be given to the people in that day:

Then certain of the scribes and of the Pharisees answered, saying, Master, we would see a sign from thee. But he answered and said unto them, An evil and adulterous generation seeketh after a sign; and there shall no sign be given to it, but the sign of the prophet Jonas: Matthew 12:39

He did so again in Matthew chapter

sixteen thus emphasizing the message. He was the almond rod that would bud and spring to resurrection life. He was the Branch that would 'rebuild the temple':

Then answered the Jews and said unto him, What sign shewest thou unto us, seeing that thou doest these things? Jesus answered and said unto them, Destroy this temple, and three days I will raise it up. John 2:19

Here He is emphatically telling them that he will be resurrected after three days, but sadly, they don't understand. Even His own disciples didn't comprehend what he was telling them.

From that time forth began Jesus to shew unto his disciples, how that he must go unto Jerusalem, and suffer many things of the elders and chief priests and scribes, and be killed, and be raised again the third day. Matthew 16:21

Jesus repeatedly said 'he who has an ear to hear, let him hear'. This was due to the fact that He had over and over given them clues in the very prophetic symbols they held dearest as to what His eventual role would be and how His ministry would play out in their sight.

However the disciples didn't understand until after the resurrection:

Then opened he their understanding, that they might understand the scriptures, And said unto them, Thus it is written, and thus it behoved Christ to suffer, and to rise from the dead the third day: And that repentance and remission of sins should be preached in his name among all nations, beginning at Jerusalem. And ye are witnesses of these things. Luke 24:45-48

Now that the disciples 'got it', they began to carry out the program He had given them in Matthew 16:19 (just before He told them in verse 21 that He would be crucified!)

Just as the almond tree was the first tree to bud, blossom and bear fruit, His was a mission to be as Romans says:

... the firstborn among many brethren.
Romans 8:29b

First Corinthians emphasizes it even more clearly:

But now is Christ risen from the dead, and become the firstfruits of them that slept. For since by man came death, by man came also the resurrection of the dead. For as in Adam all die, even so in Christ shall all be made alive.
1 Corinthians 15:21-22

The ultimate covenant symbol, the almond tree has indeed budded, blossomed, and has born fruit for two millennia. The message not only of the cross, but of the resurrection power it purchased which is the central theme of the gospel.

And God hath both raised up the Lord, and will also raise up us by his own power. 1 Corinthians 6:14

The book of Romans puts it even more powerfully:

But if the Spirit of him that raised up Jesus from the dead dwell in you, he that raised up Christ from the dead shall also quicken your mortal bodies by his Spirit that dwelleth in you. Romans 8:11

Three covenant trees give us hope for our inheritance as saints: restoration and redemption in this life, and the promise of resurrection to enter eternity with our Lord.

For the grace of God that bringeth salvation hath appeared to all men,

Teaching us that, denying ungodliness and worldly lusts, we should live soberly, righteously, and godly, in this present world; Looking for that blessed hope, and the glorious appearing of the great God and our Saviour Jesus Christ... Titus 2:12-13

Water to Wine

Spiritual Photosynthesis

Introduction

And the third day there was a marriage in Cana of Galilee; and the mother of Jesus was there: and both Jesus was called, and his disciples, to the marriage. And when they wanted wine, the mother of Jesus saith unto him, They have no wine. Jesus saith unto her, Woman, what have I to do with thee? mine hour is not yet come. His mother saith unto the servants, Whatsoever he saith unto you, do it. And there were set there six waterpots of stone, after the manner of the purifying of the Jews, containing two or three firkins apiece. Jesus saith unto them, Fill the waterpots with water. And they filled them up to the brim. And he saith unto them, Draw out now, and bear unto the governor of the feast. And they bare it. When the ruler of the feast had tasted the water that was made wine, and knew not whence it was: (but the servants which drew the water knew;) the governor of the feast called the bridegroom, And saith unto him, Every man at the beginning doth set forth good wine; and when men have well drunk, then that which is worse: but thou hast kept the good wine until now. This beginning of miracles did Jesus in Cana of Galilee, and manifested forth his glory; and his disciples believed on him. John 2:1-11

I have read, studied, and taught on this passage for decades; but a recent revisit during my morning devotional time led me on a journey that revolutionized my understanding of this familiar and unforgettable text. I have for many years reduced these verses to a symbolic treatise on the salvation experience: empty man, filled with water (the word), and the Savior's touch produces the incomparable wine of salvation. Now I began to sense something much deeper. This was a living object lesson, not only pertaining to salvation, but a view into the very nature of how God works in man, and is a picture we have been painted in the most basic chemical transaction in nature: photosynthesis. Romans 1:20 tells us:

For the invisible things of him from the creation of the world are clearly seen...

In these pages I want to decode this masterpiece of biblical symbolism showing that all the elements of photosynthesis are present in the performing of Jesus' first miracle; demonstrating the interacting of God the Father, Son, and Holy Spirit with man.

Earth

In Genesis 1 we are presented the narrative of creation. Six days God worked in the creation of all the heavens and earth; then he rested on the seventh day. Genesis 2 then offers a more detailed account of the final days of creation including the forming of man from the dust of the earth.

And every plant of the field before it was in the earth, and every herb of the field before it grew: for the LORD God had not caused it to rain upon the earth, and there was not a man to till the ground. But there went up a mist from the earth, and watered the whole face of the ground. And the LORD God formed man of the dust of the ground, and breathed into his nostrils the breath of life; and man became a living soul. Gen 2:5-7

God created man: 'Adawm' in his own likeness and image we are told. The name affixed to this man: Adam, could literally be translated 'red earth'. Based on scriptural evidence describing God in anthropomorphic (human-like) terms, it is deduced that man was created to reflect God's likeness not only in nature and character, but in appearance.

Unfortunately this similarity was short-lived. Genesis 3 tells the tragic story of Adam's rebellion against God's only commandment to Eve and himself. This sin is discovered, confronted and judged.

And unto Adam he said, Because thou hast hearkened unto the voice of thy wife, and hast eaten of the tree, of which I commanded thee, saying, Thou shalt not eat of it: cursed is the ground for thy sake; in sorrow shalt thou eat of it all the days of thy life; Thorns also and thistles shall it bring forth to thee; and thou shalt eat the herb of the field; In the sweat of thy face shalt thou eat bread, till thou return unto the ground; for out of it wast thou taken: for dust thou art, and unto dust shalt thou return. And Adam called his wife's name Eve; because she was the mother of all living. Gen 3:17-20

The ultimate judgment declared for Adam, a fate to be shared by all his offspring, was to return to the dust via the process of death and decay. Ecclesiastes gives us an even more concise picture of how this works:

Then shall the dust return to the earth as it was: and the spirit shall return unto God who gave it. Eccl 12:7

In 1 Corinthians, Paul brings the concept into 'New Testament' context by making the comparison and contrast to Christ.

And so it is written, The first man Adam was made a living soul; the last Adam was made a quickening spirit. Howbeit that was not first which is spiritual, but that which is natural; and afterward that which is spiritual. The first man is of the earth, earthy: the second man is the Lord from heaven. 1 Cor 15:45-47

Here we are told that the 'first man Adam' was of the earth and earthy. The word 'earth' here denotes tillable, cultivated ground. In fact the Greek word Adam means red earth. The word for 'earthy' is 'choikos' and means to throw down or heap up earth. It is a description reminiscent of the picture in Isaiah 64:8:

But now, O LORD, thou art our father; we are the clay, and thou our potter; and we all are the work of thy hand.

Now we have a better understanding of the picture presented in John 2 of the stone (stoneware i.e. earthen) pots. Six uniformly represents the number of man in scripture. This living parable depicts the work of God in man. This shows us the first and most basic element in photosynthesis: earth. No plant can grow or even begin life without it. It is the foundation of all that follows. As this story unfolds the other ingredients of the formula will be added one by one.

Water

The second necessary ingredient for photosynthesis is water. In scripture the water represents God's word. In Ephesians Paul gives us a beautiful picture of Christ cleansing his bride:

Husbands, love your wives, even as Christ also loved the church, and gave himself for it; That he might sanctify and cleanse it with the washing of water by the word, That he might present it to himself a glorious church, not having spot, or wrinkle... Ephesians 5:25-27

Notice the phrase 'washing of water by the word'. This clearly identifies the 'water' with his word. Not only does the water represent the word but not just any water will do. In the Torah, and the Jewish beliefs derived from its teachings, the water used for ceremonial cleansing and offerings must be living, i.e. flowing water. In fact, every ancient

Jewish mikvah or baptismal had at least a trickle of running water flowing into it. Notice the phrasing of Jeremiah's condemnation of Israel for their spiritual abandonment of God.

For my people have committed two evils; they have forsaken me the fountain of living waters, and hewed them out cisterns, broken cisterns, that can hold no water. Jer 2:13

When Jesus talked with the woman at Jacob's well he used the same symbolism; contrasting the natural water from the well to the living water of his word.

Now Jacob's well was there. Jesus therefore, being wearied with his journey, sat thus on the well: and it was about the sixth hour. There cometh a woman of Samaria to draw water: Jesus saith unto her, Give me to drink. (For his disciples were gone away unto the city to buy meat.) Then saith the woman of Samaria unto him, How is it that thou, being a Jew, askest drink of me, which am a woman of Samaria? for the Jews have no dealings with the Samaritans. Jesus answered and said unto her, If thou knewest the gift of God, and who it is that saith to thee, Give me to drink; thou wouldest have asked of him, and he would have given thee living water. The woman saith unto him, Sir, thou hast nothing to draw with, and the well is deep: from whence then hast thou that living water? Art thou greater than our father Jacob, which gave us the well, and drank thereof himself, and his children, and his cattle? Jesus answered and said unto her, Whosoever drinketh of this water shall thirst again: But whosoever drinketh of the water that I shall give him shall never thirst; but the water that I shall give him shall be in him a well of water springing up into everlasting life. John 4:6-14

Here we recognize the second element of God's miracle of photosynthesis: living water. When Jesus was about to perform his first miracle he instructed the servants to fill the pots to the brim. This entailed pouring in water; hence it was living (flowing) water. We now see earthen vessels filled up with living water. The vessels are ready for the next necessary ingredient.

Air

The third element required for photosynthesis is air. It is vital to understand this part of the formula to know that the Greek word for air, 'pneuma', is also the same word translated 'spirit'. The Hebrew wording is similar. The two Old Testament words translated breath: neshamah and ruach, are also translated spirit! As we have already seen in Genesis 2:7 God breathed into man the breath (neshamah) of life and he became a living soul. In verse 19 we see a contrast in that God formed all the animals out of the ground (adamah) just like he did Adam but did not give them the neshamah or spirit of life.

We see this contrast taken to the next logical step in one of the verses from 1 Corinthians 15 quoted in chapter 1.

And so it is written, The first man Adam was made a living soul; the last Adam was made a quickening spirit.
1 Cor 15:45

Notice that Adam was superior to the animals in that he had a living spirit <u>from God</u>, but Christ was infinitely superior to Adam in the he was indwelt by the Holy Spirit <u>of God</u>.

We see this principle highlighted in the words of John the Baptist as he spoke to his disciples:

He that cometh from above is above all: he that is of the earth is earthly, and speaketh of the earth: he that cometh from heaven is above all. And what he hath seen and heard, that he testifieth; and no man receiveth his testimony. He that hath received his testimony hath set to his seal that God is true. For he whom God hath sent speaketh the words of God: for God giveth not the Spirit by measure unto him. The Father loveth the Son, and hath given all things into his hand. John 3:31-35

In this passage we are told that Jesus was not given the Spirit by measure. The Father had given 'all things' into his hand. This is a 'game-changer'. Under the old covenant the earth (man) and the water (word) were present but not this indwelt power of the Holy Spirit. Notice that Jesus neither touched the water pots nor even spoke to them. He took no action at all! Merely his presence with the measureless Spirit within him instantly changed the water to wine.

In the next two chapters we will see the process unfold whereby this action, this 'spiritual photosynthesis', takes place.

Catalyst

In the earthly, natural process of photosynthesis, the basic elements: earth, water, and air must always be present for the chemical reactions that produce life-giving nutrition to the plant to operate. There is, however one additional ingredient that must be present or the other compounds will simply sit in the plant cells and remain totally inert. That key chemical ingredient is chlorophyll; the substance that gives all plants their green coloring. The chlorophyll, though undergoing no change in its own structure, enables the other chemical compounds to interact and combine to produce one substance, and one substance only: sugar. The fuel for all life is created only when this essential part of the formula is present.

In spiritual terms, what then is the 'catalyst' of releasing miraculous power such as we see in John 2? It is God's will. We can have all the elements necessary come together: earth (man), water (word), and air (Spirit); but if an action is not in line with the Father's will all will be for nothing. God's sovereign will is the catalyst for operation in his kingdom. Even Jesus, whom we saw in the last chapter was given the Spirit without measure, would not and could not operate independent of the father's will.

Notice his conversation with his mother in John 2:

And the third day there was a marriage in Cana of Galilee; and the mother of Jesus was there: And both Jesus was called, and his disciples, to the marriage. And when they wanted wine, the mother of Jesus saith unto him, They have no wine. Jesus saith unto her, Woman, what have I to do with thee? mine hour is not yet come. His mother saith unto the servants, Whatsoever he saith unto you, do it. John 2:1-5

He actually hesitates and questions her; '...what have I to do with thee? mine hour is not yet come.' Here he is caught between obeying his Father's will and honoring his mother's request. From the rest of the narrative it is obvious that this action ultimately met with the Father's approval. Mary, sensing this, immediately instructed the servants: 'Whatsoever he saith unto you, do it.'

This is a key point to the manner in which Jesus operated in his earthly ministry. He was in lock step with God's will. In fact, he makes an astounding statement in John 5:

Then answered Jesus and said unto them, Verily, verily, I say unto you, The Son can do nothing of himself, but what he seeth the Father do: for what things soever he doeth, these also doeth the Son likewise. John 5:19

Here we see Jesus' fundamental

philosophy and mode of operation: whatever the Father does, Jesus does. This also highlights another important point. Jesus sensed and knew what his Father was **going to do** and aligned his actions and ministry to match. This emphasizes the importance of Paul's admonition:

For as many as are led by the Spirit of God, they are the sons of God. Romans 8:14

All our actions, therefore, must be first agreeable to God's word; and then, must be in alignment with his will. Christians are fond of quoting Matthew 28:18:

And Jesus came and spake unto them, saying, All power is given unto me in heaven and in earth. Matt 28:18

However, it is crucial to note that this statement was made only **after** his earthly ministry was completed and he was about to ascend into heaven to begin his heavenly ministry as our 'great high priest' as Paul puts it. Before this juncture he was operating in his earthly ministry, in his human incarnation, just as we as believers do with one exception. We are not given the spirit without measure. Jesus, like us, was a fully human man operating within the parameters of the Father's will by the operation of the Holy Spirit anointing on him (Christ is from the Greek Christos which means anointed one) according to God's word. This order and alignment released the power of God to do all the mighty works Jesus accomplished during his earthly ministry. As we will see in the following chapter, that mission has been passed on to us!

Power

In photosynthesis, while it is true that without the chlorophyll no chemical action takes place, it is equally true that without an energy source, i.e. the sun, there is nothing to power the chemical process. So we see that God's will and God's power work hand-in-hand. Without his power nothing spiritual happens; outside his will nothing spiritual is allowed to happen. Without the catalyst our efforts are inert; without the Spirit they are dead.

Just as we cycle through periods of daylight and nighttime, there are times and seasons in God's flow of anointing according to his will. We see in Jesus life and ministry that there were times and seasons. Remember in our text he says to Mary 'mine hour is not yet come...'. We see an ebb and flow of miracles and events:

For the Father loveth the Son, and sheweth him all things that himself doeth: and he will shew him greater works than these, that ye may marvel. John 5:20

God revealed his plan and then worked it through Christ; sometimes in teaching and sometimes in great power. As we see above there were times of greater power and miracles. It works the same way for us as believers. In fact, he makes an astounding statement in John 14:

Believe me that I am in the Father, and the Father in me: or else believe me for the very works' sake. Verily, verily, I say unto you, He that believeth on me, the works that I do shall he do also; and greater works than these shall he do; because I go unto my Father. And whatsoever ye shall ask in my name, that will I do, that the Father may be glorified in the Son. John 14:11-13

Here we see that in God's timing and season **we** were chosen to display his power by 'greater works' than Jesus. Not greater in magnitude, but greater in scope and number simply because we can be all over the globe at any one instant in time. We have more opportunities to minster and demonstrate his power. This was the Lord's plan all along as Paul writes in Romans 8:

And we know that all things work together for good to them that love God, to them who are the called according to his purpose. For whom he did foreknow, he also did predestinate to be conformed to the image of his Son, that he might be the firstborn among many brethren. Moreover whom he did predestinate, them he also called: and whom he called, them he also justified: and whom he justified, them he also glorified. What shall we then say to these things? If God be for us, who can be against us? Romans 8:29-31

God routinely gives us opportunities to reach out to unbelievers, minister to the sick and hurting, and to comfort those who are in need; whether physical, emotional, or spiritual. We must look for and recognize those 'God moments' and not miss them because those are the instances in which we are most likely to have the greatest success. Think about it: if the Lord orchestrates such an encounter we can feel assured that his will is being met and his power will show up! All pressure is off of us; we must simply seize the moment and act in obedience to God's word. The rest is totally up to him.

Fruit

As we have seen the process of photosynthesis is unique in its complexity of design, and yet is ultimately very simple in its operation. Supply the plant with earth, water, and air; add sunlight and the catalytic action of the chlorophyll combines carbon dioxide from the air with water from the soil and creates simple sugar in the plant cells. The sugar provides energy to fuel the ongoing cell processes of the plant, but it also fulfills another need that is crucial to the survival of the plant species: it is the stuff of which fruit is made.

All plants reproduce by means of seed-bearing fruit. Some have more sugar inside (sweeter) and some less. This sugar is the power plant to energize the seeds when its time for them to germinate. It also is enticing to animals and birds which eat the fruit and then spread the seeds. Genesis 1 tells us:

And God said, Let the earth bring forth grass, the herb yielding seed, and the fruit tree yielding fruit after his kind, whose seed is in itself, upon the earth: and it was so. And the earth brought forth grass, and herb yielding seed after his kind, and the tree yielding fruit, whose seed is in itself. Gen 1:12

Notice that the fruit contains the seed. If there is no fruit produced there is no seed to propagate the plant species. Now we get an inkling of the importance of Jesus' statement:

Abide in me, and I in you. As the branch cannot bear fruit of itself, except it abide in the vine; no more can ye, except ye abide in me. I am the vine, ye are the branches: He that abideth in me, and I in him, the same bringeth forth much fruit: for without me ye can do nothing. John 15:5

Only to the extent we abide in him allowing the power of the Holy Spirit to flow through us can we bear fruit. The goal is stated here that we bear 'much fruit'. The fruit, however is not an end in itself. It is merely a vehicle to contain and carry the seed! Galatians 5 tells us:

But the fruit of the Spirit is love, joy, peace, longsuffering, gentleness, goodness, faith, Meekness, temperance: against such there is no law. Gal 5:23

If we are to bear the fruit of the Spirit, and according to Genesis 1 the pattern God established is for the seed to be in the fruit; then it stands to reason that if we are bearing no fruit then we have **no seed to plant**! Just as the plant cannot reproduce without seed, we as believers cannot reproduce ourselves by leading new believers into the kingdom unless we have the fruit of the Spirit dropping from our daily lives. Studies and polls show that the huge majority of unchurched individuals do not attend church because they see no benefit in it. Fruitless Christians lack any enticement for them. However, believers that routinely display and distribute the sweetness of the fruit of the Spirit produce a spiritual hunger in those they interact with. It is a natural progression as St. Francis of Assisi stated centuries ago: "go into all the world and preach the Gospel, and if necessary, use words...".

Paul lays out the process in 1 Corinthians 3:

Who then is Paul, and who is Apollos, but ministers by whom ye believed, even as the Lord gave to every man? I have planted, Apollos watered; but God gave the increase. So then neither is he that planteth any thing, neither he that watereth; but God that giveth the increase. Now he that planteth and he that watereth are one: and every man shall receive his own reward according to his own labour. For we are labourers together with God: ye are God's husbandry, ye are God's building. 1 Cor 3:5-9

Paul says that he sowed, (in the earth) Apollos watered, (supplied the water of the word) and God (within his will and empowered by his Spirit) gives the increase (the harvest of souls).

Conclusion

I realize it is easy to get caught up in the technical terms regarding the photosynthesis system and lose sight of the lessons contained in one of God's greatest miracles of creation. It is essential, however to grasp that this process is a living picture of how our Christian lives and personal ministries should look. This concept should not be foreign to us. Paul states in Romans 1:

For the wrath of God is revealed from heaven against all ungodliness and unrighteousness of men, who hold the truth in unrighteousness; Because that which may be known of God is manifest in them; for God hath shewed it unto them. For the invisible things of him from the creation of the world are clearly seen, being understood by the things that are made, even his eternal power and Godhead; so that they are without excuse: Romans 1:18-20

Here we are plainly told that the power of God, his plans, purposes, and nature can be clearly seen and understood, **even by unbelievers**. If the Lord went to such lengths to display his unfathomable wisdom by building it into every act of creation; we must not overlook or fail to recognize the beautiful spiritual object lessons he is providing for us. Similarly, Jesus ministered in such a way that each of his miracles and teachings not only consisted of their face-value meaning, but they also painted a picture based on the Old Testament law, prophecies, and teachings. Let's re-examine Jesus first miracle in light of this revelation.

First we must realize that we as believers are the water pots.

For God, who commanded the light to shine out of darkness, hath shined in our hearts, to give the light of the knowledge of the glory of God in the face of Jesus Christ. But we have this treasure in earthen vessels, that the excellency of the power may be of God, and not of us. 2 Cor 4:7

Notice that not only are we the vessels made of earth, but that we are created for a specific purpose: to be filled with water. Next, we see that we are to be 'filled to the brim' with the water of the word. We should have a regular, at least daily, encounter with our heavenly Father in his word. Third, we are to be in complete subjection to God's will:

I beseech you therefore, brethren, by the mercies of God, that ye present your bodies a living sacrifice, holy, acceptable unto God, which is your reasonable service. And be not conformed to this world: but be ye transformed by the renewing of your mind, that ye may prove what is that good, and acceptable, and perfect, will of God. Romans 12:1-2

Lastly, we must allow his Holy Spirit to fill and flow though us so as to activate and empower the spiritual 'photosynthesis' within us to produce the fruit of the Spirit and draws others to Christ.

See then that ye walk circumspectly, not as fools, but as wise, Redeeming the time, because the days are evil. Wherefore be ye not unwise, but understanding what the will of the Lord is. And be not drunk with wine, wherein is excess; but be filled with the Spirit... Eph 5:16-18

God then requires our availability, our connected fellowship, our submission to his will, and our participation in his plans for our lives and the lives of others. Remember Jesus' admonition:

I am the true vine... Abide in me...

Four Pillars for Your Day

Chapter One
Set Your Day in Order

Too many times, we as believers rise in the morning and set off on our day without giving any thought to what we are going to do, what we want or need to accomplish, or even <u>why</u> we are doing what we do. This helter-skelter approach to our daily walk is an open door for Satan to gain entrance and wreck our lives. God is a God of order and His plans have been laid out from everlasting.

Known unto God are all his works from the beginning of the world.
Acts 15:18 KJV

...That it might be fulfilled which was spoken by the prophet, saying, I will open my mouth in parables; I will utter things which have been kept secret from the foundation of the world. Matt 13:35 KJV

God's plans for us have been established in His omniscient mind from eternity past, including our salvation; Revelation 13:8 calls Christ *'the Lamb slain from the foundation of the world.'* In fact, God's will for our lives has been appointed before our birth.

The Lord called me before I was born, while I was in my mother's womb He named me. Isaiah 49:1 CEV

...we know that all things work together for good to them that love God, to them who are the called according to his purpose. For whom he did foreknow, he also did predestinate to be conformed to the image of his Son...
Romans 8:28-29 KJV

Since God has definite plans for us, we should submit to Him and His will for us.

In all thy ways acknowledge him, and he shall direct thy paths. Proverbs 3:6 KJV

For I know the plans that I have for you, declares the LORD, plans for welfare and not for calamity to give you a future and a hope. Jeremiah 29:11 NAS

His plans for us are good and filled with blessings. We have only to let Him work them out in our lives to achieve and receive all He has for us.

We also have to recognize that His plans are vastly superior to anything we can devise and that He will ensure their successful conclusion. The Lord will work out his plans for my life. Psalms 138:8 Living

For the Lord watches over all the plans and paths of godly men, but the paths of the godless lead to doom. Psalm 1:6 KJV

This however, doesn't mean that we are robots who have no will or mind; but that we must plan and approach our lives with His will and leading in mind.

The mind of man plans his way, But the Lord directs his steps. Proverbs 16:9 NAS

There is an old adage that says "we have to work like it all depends on us and pray like it all depends on God." This is never more true than in this instance. We do our best and follow the leadership of the Holy Spirit and leave the results with Him.

We can make our plans, but the final outcome is in God's hands. Proverbs 16:1 Living

Recognizing and following God's will and plans brings order to our otherwise chaotic lives. Just as reading Genesis chapter 1 gives us a view of God bringing order to the chaos of the newly created universe.

Psalm 37:23 says:

The steps of a good man are ordered by

the LORD: and he delighteth in his way.

If God has chosen to order our steps; i.e. to set in order our path, then it is only logical to assume we should do the same. If we are to follow His plans, we have to have a working knowledge of what those plans are based on; what the scripture reveals to us of His will and nature. We can then pray those things into our lives by praying the relevant scriptures over ourselves. This type of prayer can NEVER fail since it is automatically in God's perfect will. We can often miss His will for our lives by doing and even praying wrong things; however we can never fail when we pray scripture. (unless of course, we take it out of context and twist it into something He never intended it to say and to be) Psalm 19 records a prayer for the psalmist's words to be in line with God's will and desires:

Keep back thy servant also from presumptuous sins; let them not have dominion over me: then shall I be upright, and I shall be innocent from the great transgression. Let the words of my mouth, and the meditation of my heart, be acceptable in thy sight, O LORD, my strength, and my redeemer. Psalms 19:13-4 KJV

This passage tells us firstly that we have to avoid presumptuous sins. This means that we can't presume to set our own course. James 4:13-14 warns us not to declare what we will do in the future because we don't know what our lives will be like tomorrow. The second message in this scripture is the desire of the psalmist to have his thoughts, desires, and words of prayer to be 'acceptable' to the Lord. This again can be ensured by praying scripture. Deuteronomy chapter six gives us a primer on this subject:

Now these are the commandments, the statutes, and the judgments, which the LORD your God commanded to teach you, that ye might do them in the land whither ye go to possess it: That thou mightiest fear the LORD thy God, to keep all his statutes and his commandments, which I command thee, thou, and thy son, and thy son's son, all the days of thy life; and that thy days may be prolonged. Hear therefore, O Israel, and observe to do it; that it may be well with thee, and that ye may increase mightily, as the LORD God of thy fathers hath promised thee, in the land that floweth with milk and honey. Hear, O Israel: The LORD our God is one LORD: And thou shalt love the LORD thy God with all thine heart, and with all thy soul, and with all thy might. And these words, which I command thee this day, shall be in thine heart: And thou shalt teach them diligently unto thy children, and shalt talk of them when thou sittest in thine house, and when thou walkest by the way, and when thou liest down, and when thou risest up. And thou shalt bind them for a sign upon thine hand, and they shall be as frontlets between thine eyes. And thou shalt write them upon the posts of thy house, and on thy gates. Deut 6:1-9 KJV

In the time that this passage was written, there was no written scripture. It was passed down from generation to generation by oral repetition such as is described in the verses above. However, this also had the effect of putting it in their hearts as the verses indicate; and it also had the by-product of having them continually speaking, i.e. praying the scriptures over themselves and their families.

This principle is just as valid and just as beneficial today as it was nearly five thousand years ago when these words were given to Moses by God Himself. The spiritual discipline of praying scripture is very fruitful for any believer and it is the purpose of this small book to give you four key passages to pray over yourself at the beginning of every single day to 'set your day in order'.

Chapter Two
The Proclamation

The first pillar is based on Psalm 103. This pillar is what I call the proclamation. It is a declaration of who we are in God's eyes and how He looks at and interacts with us.

Bless the LORD, O my soul: and all that is within me, bless his holy name. Bless the LORD, O my soul, and forget not all his benefits: Who forgiveth all thine iniquities; who healeth all thy diseases; Who redeemeth thy life from destruction; who crowneth thee with lovingkindness and tender mercies; Who satisfieth thy mouth with good things; so that thy youth is renewed like the eagle's. The LORD executeth righteousness and judgment for all that are oppressed. Psalms 103:1-6 KJV

This first section of this chapter exhorts

us to 'Bless the LORD' and to not forget all His benefits. It then proceeds to name them: forgiveness, healing, redemption, loving kindness, and mercy. We are also told that he will satisfy (fill) our mouths with good things to renew our youth. What an awesome promise to start your day on! It goes on to say that He will execute righteousness and judgment for us when we are oppressed; in other words, God is going to watch over us and take up for us.

The next section tells us how God looks at us in regard to our failings.

The LORD is merciful and gracious, slow to anger, and plenteous in mercy. He will not always chide: neither will he keep his anger for ever. He hath not dealt with us after our sins; nor rewarded us according to our iniquities. For as the heaven is high above the earth, so great is his mercy toward them that fear him. As far as the east is from the west, so far hath he removed our transgressions from us. Like as a father pitieth his children, so the LORD pitieth them that fear him. For he knoweth our frame; he remembereth that we are dust. Psalms 103:9-14 KJV

This passage shows us clearly that God, far from being a tyrant that is ever ready to pounce on us for every misstep, is actually a loving Father who wants us to be Holy. However He acknowledges the fact that we are fallen, imperfect creatures and will never be sinless this side of eternity. Verse 10 states that He doesn't deal with us according to our sins and rebellion. Instead, verse 13 tells us that He pities us like a father does an unruly child; wanting only to discipline and teach the child for its own good. The capstone of the passage is the revelation that He remembers that we are dust; we are only fallen, mortal men.

The next section of the passage acknowledges the fleeting nature of man's existence in this world, but reiterates the eternal nature of God's mercy and righteousness toward us:

As for man, his days are as grass: as a flower of the field, so he flourisheth. For the wind passeth over it, and it is gone; and the place thereof shall know it no more. But the mercy of the LORD is from everlasting to everlasting upon them that fear him, and his righteousness unto children's children; To such as keep his covenant, and to those that remember his commandments to do them. Psalms 103:16-18 KJV

This pillar chapter reminds us that in spite of our human failings, God has only our best in mind and looks on us from that viewpoint. He treats us with grace and mercy, not judgment, and this is the key to our proclamation to build our day. It is a heaven's eye look at how He sees us that sets the tone for the rest of the pillars. It is the foundation stone on which all the others rest. If we have a dysfunctional view of how God sees us and relates to us, we can never stand in faith to receive the rest of His promises. This chapter gives us that faith foundation on which to proclaim our status as beloved children of the Most High with thankfulness and confidence. It is important to not only believe these things, but to speak them out in a proclamation of faith. In Mark chapter 11 Jesus stresses the importance of these declarations or proclamations.

*"Truly I say to you, whoever **says** to this mountain, 'be taken up and cast into the sea,' and does not doubt in his heart, but believes what he **says** is going to happen, it will be granted him. "Therefore I say to you, all things for which you pray and ask, believe that you have received them, and they will be granted you." Mark 11:23-24 NAS (emphasis mine)*

Begin your day with a proclamation of who and what you are in God, and believe you receive the promises of these pillar chapters and they WILL be yours!

Chapter Three
The Preparation

The second pillar is Ephesians chapter six. This passage is very familiar to many Christians as the 'armor of God' chapter. Once we have made our proclamation and laid the cornerstone of our daily walk, we must make preparation to carry out our mission as a soldier in the army of the Lord. Ephesians six begins by discussing our service for God and the attitude we are to maintain in our relationships with others. It then begins in verse 10 to talk about the warfare we are in on a daily basis.

Finally, my brethren, be strong in the Lord, and in the power of his might. Put on the whole armour of God, that ye may be able to stand against the wiles of the devil. For we wrestle not against flesh and blood, but against principalities, against powers, against the rulers of the darkness of this world, against spiritual wickedness in high places. Ephesians 6:10-12 KJV

This passage clearly indicates that we:

1] are in a struggle/battle
2] it is against dark spiritual forces
3] the enemy has plans to attack and defeat us

We are admonished to 'be strong in the Lord' as our way of preparation for victory . Verse 11 tells us to 'put on the full armor'; it is only when we are fully equipped can we be assured of victory. Our strength is insufficient, but His strength is all sufficient. We are further told that it is by the 'strength of His might'. The Greek word translated strength is 'kratos' which means more than just strength or power; it has a connotation of strength in dominion and authority. The word translated might, 'ischus', can also be rendered as ability. Just take a second look at this verse from that viewpoint; "be strong in the

Lord and in the dominion of His ability". He is Almighty and His dominion is unchallenged, so when we go out to battle in our daily walk relying on His ability and the dominion He has through His omnipotence; there is no obstacle too great for us. The preparation detailed in the next few verses puts us in the position to walk in that ability and dominion;

"Christ in you, the hope of glory". Colossians 1:27 KJV

Wherefore take unto you the whole armour of God, that ye may be able to withstand in the evil day, and having done all, to stand. Stand therefore, having your loins girt about with truth, and having on the breastplate of righteousness; And your feet shod with the preparation of the gospel of peace; Above all, taking the shield of faith, wherewith ye shall be able to quench all the fiery darts of the wicked. And take the helmet of salvation, and the sword of the Spirit, which is the word of God: Eph 6:14-17 KJV

Here we are told once again to take 'the whole armor'. Each piece is as necessary as any other and as each piece is added to the whole, our ability to cope with whatever the enemy throws at us becomes more complete. Virtually all the references to the individual pieces of armor are quotes from the Old Testament; particularly Isaiah's writings. They are all from Messianic prophecies. This shows us that just as Jesus walked and fought the devil in this armor we are to follow His example.

The first piece of armor is the belt of truth. We have to be honest and transparent both with God and with those around us. This short-circuits Satan's attempts to get us to walk in deception; even self-deception. It also helps us avoid temptations. Satan knows as well as we do what our weak points are and will repeatedly try to exploit them. By being transparent with even a few key brothers and/or sisters we can have a level of accountability that will help us stand up to many everyday temptations and snares of the enemy.

Iron sharpeneth iron; so a man sharpeneth the countenance of his friend. Proverbs 27:17

The next piece of armor is the breastplate of righteousness. Just as the breastplate covers your vital organs, walking in accord with God's statutes is a protection against the most devastating of Satan's attacks. This also ties in with the third pillar of protection which will be discussed in the next chapter.

We also must have the shoes of the Gospel on our feet. This is obviously directly related to our Christian walk. We must know and apply the word in our everyday life to be successful. Hosea 4:6

says:

My people are destroyed for lack of knowledge.

We cannot overcome in a battle in which we don't know where the battle lines are drawn. The Apostle Paul likens it to a sporting event in which we are striving for victory.

Follow the Lord's rules for doing his work, just as an athlete either follows the rules or is disqualified and wins no prize. II Timothy 2:5 Living

We must know the rules of engagement if we are to follow them and gain ultimate victory. Notice also that it is called the Gospel of peace. Walking in His ways brings peace and contentment to our lives.

The next item of armor is the shield of faith. The shield is our first line of defense against the enemy. It is faith that we are told will not only deflect but extinguish the fiery darts of his attacks. Faith is the agent in our lives that activates all the other weapons at our disposal, both offensive and defensive. The shield also covers up for many of the shortcomings and chinks in our other armor.

We are also told to put on the helmet of salvation. This doesn't refer to our eternal salvation, but speaks of the covering of our head; i.e. our mind. This is the battleground of most of Satan's attacks. We are told to 'renew our minds.' (Romans 12:2) The salvation spoken of here is the renewing and transforming of our minds as we learn and grow in Him.

Finally, we are told to take the sword of the Spirit. It is His sword, not ours. We are to wield it as He directs. Notice in Luke chapter 4 that as Satan tries to tempt Christ the response is always "it is written". Christ battered Satan at every turn with the Word until the enemy had to retreat from the battle.

Verse 18 gives us the last ingredient; prayer. If the Word is the power source, then prayer is the switch! Prayer energizes our faith and the Word as we speak it out and confront Satan.

Chapter Four
The Protection

The third pillar chapter is Psalm 91. This chapter contains what are some of the best and most recognized verses on protection in the entire body of scripture. It also speaks of an intimate relationship with our heavenly Father. The two go hand-in-hand. The first few lines of this Psalm show us a glimpse of God as a loving Father who covers us with His protection.

He that dwelleth in the secret place of the most High shall abide under the shadow of the Almighty. Surely he shall deliver thee from the snare of the fowler ... He shall cover thee with his feathers, and under his wings shalt thou trust Psalms 91:1;3a;4a KJV

Here we see God depicted as a parent bird protecting its young. He will literally hide us from the traps of the hunter (Satan) as long as we dwell in His secret place. The reference to His wings can also be translated from the Hebrew as border, corner, or skirts and is considered by many rabbinical scholars to refer to the tallit or prayer shawl. From this viewpoint we get a picture of God shading us with a canopy formed by His heavenly tallit protecting us from any attack by the enemy.

We also see a more military aspect of His protection.

I will say of the LORD, He is my refuge and my fortress: my God; in him will I trust ... his truth shall be thy shield and buckler. Psalm 91:2;4b KJV

As I mentioned in the last chapter these verses resonate with the armor of God passage in Ephesians chapter 6. Remember that it is called the **armor of God**. Here we see that although we must take it to ourselves, He is the one who empowers and enforces its protection.

The following verse of Psalm 91 gives us a whole list of perils that we are immune from in His protection:

... from the noisome pestilence ... Thou shalt not be afraid for the terror by night; nor for the arrow that flieth by day; Nor for the pestilence that wasteth at noonday. Psalm 3b,5-6 KJV

In these verses it is obvious that ALL types of attack are covered: both day and night, whether mental--terror by night, physical—pestilence/noisome pestilence or financial--destruction that wasteth (or spoils). All avenues of assault on our lives are dealt with, leaving no open avenue to the enemy ... as long as we abide, continue, and remain in His presence and protection.

The passage continues with a promise that though many around us will fall prey to the enemy and suffer, we will be immune. (There is one caveat to this; we are NEVER promised immunity to or protection from spiritual persecution.) It also includes a promise that we will eventually see the judgment and punishment of all our enemies—this includes Satan himself.

Only with thine eyes shalt thou behold and see the reward of the wicked. Psalm 91:8 KJV

The passage then proceeds to give us a promise of direct angelic intervention into our life situations.

Because thou hast made the LORD, which is my refuge, even the most High, thy habitation; There shall no evil befall thee, neither shall any plague come nigh thy dwelling. For he shall give his angels charge over thee, to keep thee in all thy ways. They shall bear thee up in their hands, lest thou dash thy foot against a stone. Psalms 91:12 KJV

The next verse gives us a promise of supernatural authority in dealing with the enemy:

Thou shalt tread upon the lion and adder: the young lion and the dragon shalt thou trample under feet. Psalm 91:13 KJV

These words are echoed by Jesus in Luke 10:18-20:

And he said unto them, I beheld Satan as lightning fall from heaven. Behold, I give unto you power to tread on serpents and scorpions, and over all the power of the enemy: and nothing shall by any means hurt you. Notwithstanding in this rejoice not, that the spirits are subject unto you; but rather rejoice, because your names are written in heaven.

This is a promise, not only of authority in spiritual warfare, but of ultimate victory in the war.

The chapter concludes with a set of

promises from God Himself:

Because he hath set his love upon me, therefore will I deliver him: I will set him on high, ...because he hath known my name. He shall call upon me, and I will answer him: I will be with him in trouble; I will deliver him, and honour him. With long life will I satisfy him, and shew him my salvation. Psalms 91:15-16 KJV

This chapter is the conclusion of what I would call the construction process. There follows in the next chapter a process that I would term the adornment.

Chapter Five
The Provision

In the first four chapters of this book we have examined the construction or building up of our daily lives. The principles based on this pillar chapter will deal with the adornment of those lives; the daily and ongoing provision for the things necessary to sustain and adorn our lives. It is plain from scriptures, both Old Testament and New Testament, that God wants His people to have not only sufficiency; but plenty. The twenty-eighth chapter of Deuteronomy is the key to a treasure trove of God's provision. Remember, these are promises made to His people over 3400 years ago and as we have already seen in Psalm 103:

But the mercy of the LORD is from everlasting to everlasting upon them that fear him, and his righteousness unto children's children; To such as keep his covenant, and to those that remember his commandments to do them.

The first two verses of this chapter set a tone that is carried on throughout the whole passage: that these promises are dependant on our obedience to His commands.

And it shall come to pass, if thou shalt hearken diligently unto the voice of the LORD thy God, to observe and to do all his commandments which I command thee this day, that the LORD thy God will set thee on high above all nations of the earth: And all these blessings shall come on thee, and overtake thee, if thou shalt hearken unto the voice of the LORD thy God. Deut 28:1-2 KJV

Notice that He first states that we must 'diligently' listen and obey; but then states that if we do the blessings will 'come on' us and 'overtake' us. It seems to be automatic; if we obey we just can't help but get blessed. We then see a long list of blessings that are coming our way:

Blessed shalt thou be in the city, and blessed shalt thou be in the field. Blessed shall be the fruit of thy body, and the fruit of thy ground, and the fruit of thy cattle, the increase of thy kine, and the flocks of thy sheep. Blessed shall be thy basket and thy store. Blessed shalt thou be when thou comest in, and blessed shalt thou be when thou goest out. Deut 28:4-6 KJV

In the time that this passage was written, the primary form of wealth came from agriculture or the trading of agricultural commodities; which were at times bartered for precious metals or stones. Notice in these verses that in addition to personal household increase (a host of children, especially sons, was considered treasure in itself; giving the family unit workers and fighters to protect their goods) nearly every form of agricultural increase, plenty, and commerce is listed. This is followed by promises of protection and blessing on them, their storage facilities, their land, and in fact, their every effort.

The LORD shall cause thine enemies that rise up against thee to be smitten before thy face: they shall come out against thee one way, and flee before thee seven ways. The LORD shall command the blessing upon thee in thy storehouses, and in all that thou settest thine hand unto; and he shall bless thee in the land which the LORD thy God giveth thee. Deut 28:8 KJV

Next the LORD calls down a blessing on them as a people; establishing and elevating their relationship to Him and their status in their world.

The LORD shall establish thee an holy people unto himself, as he hath sworn unto thee, if thou shalt keep the commandments of the LORD thy God, and walk in his ways. And all people of the earth shall see that thou art called by the name of the LORD; and they shall be afraid of thee. Deuteronomy 28:9-10

The Lord now sums up these blessings by promising them abundance; supplying them from His 'good treasure' and an exalted status among their peers:

And the LORD shall make thee plenteous in goods, in the fruit of thy body, and in the fruit of thy cattle, and in the fruit of thy ground, in the land which the LORD sware unto thy fathers to give thee. The LORD shall open unto thee his good treasure, the heaven to give the rain unto thy land in his season, and to bless all the work of thine hand: and thou shalt lend unto many nations, and thou shalt not borrow. And the LORD shall make thee the head, and not the tail; and thou shalt be above only, and thou shalt not be beneath; Deut 28:12-13a KJV

Once again, these promised blessings are dependant on our obedience:

... if that thou hearken unto the commandments of the LORD thy God, which I command thee this day, to observe and to do them: And thou shalt not go aside from any of the words which I command thee this day, to the right hand, or to the left, to go after other gods to serve them. Deut 28:13b-14 KJV

Chapter Six
The Purpose

The purpose of putting these four pillar chapters together in this format is to give you a set of scriptures to pray through on a daily basis to set your day in order and shape the spiritual atmosphere in which you live. I have personally prayed these scriptures for many years; not continually I'm afraid, and the difference is obvious when I neglect them. A personal recommitment to practice this spiritual discipline EVERY day was the seed that germinated into this little book.

These passages should be prayed every day, preferably out loud, and they should be prayed prophetically; that is, they should be recited filling in personal pronouns: I, me, my, etc. when appropriate (sometimes I even fill in my first name!). This makes them personal and puts them into our ear gate.

A man's belly shall be satisfied with the fruit of his mouth; and with the increase of his lips shall he be filled. Death and life are in the power of the tongue: and they that love it shall eat the fruit thereof. Proverbs 18:21 KJV

Notice how important the tongue is and the result of its overflow. Hearing effects what we think, what we think effects what we do, and what we do effects what we have as we have already read in Deuteronomy chapter 28. Proverbs 23:7 tells us as a man *'thinketh in his heart, so is he'*.

A good man out of the good treasure of his heart bringeth forth that which is good; and an evil man out of the evil treasure of his heart bringeth forth that which is evil: for of the abundance of the heart his mouth speaketh. Luke 6:45 KJV

What we speak with our mouth, hear with our ears, and meditate on with our mind will eventually become rooted firmly in our heart. This will create the fruit of a good heart and produce 'good treasure' in our life!

Appendix
Psalm 103:1-18

1 Bless the LORD, O my soul: and all that is within me, bless his holy name.

2 Bless the LORD, O my soul, and forget not all his benefits:

3 Who forgiveth all thine iniquities; who healeth all thy diseases;

4 Who redeemeth thy life from destruction; who crowneth thee with lovingkindness and tender mercies;

5 Who satisfieth thy mouth with good things; so that thy youth is renewed like the eagle's.

6 The LORD executeth righteousness and judgment for all that are oppressed.

7 He made known his ways unto Moses, his acts unto the children of Israel.

8 The LORD is merciful and gracious, slow to anger, and plenteous in mercy.

9 He will not always chide: neither will he keep his anger for ever.

10 He hath not dealt with us after our sins; nor rewarded us according to our iniquities.

11 For as the heaven is high above the

earth, so great is his mercy toward them that fear him.

12 As far as the east is from the west, so far hath he removed our transgressions from us.

13 Like as a father pitieth his children, so the LORD pitieth them that fear him.

14 For he knoweth our frame; he remembereth that we are dust.

15 As for man, his days are as grass: as a flower of the field, so he flourisheth.

16 For the wind passeth over it, and it is gone; and the place thereof shall know it no more.

17 But the mercy of the LORD is from everlasting to everlasting upon them that fear him, and his righteousness unto children's children;

18 To such as keep his covenant, and to those that remember his commandments to do them.

Ephesians 6:10

10 Finally, my brethren, be strong in the Lord, and in the power of his might.

11 Put on the whole armour of God, that ye may be able to stand against the wiles of the devil.

12 For we wrestle not against flesh and blood, but against principalities, against powers, against the rulers of the darkness of this world, against spiritual wickedness in high places.

13 Wherefore take unto you the whole armour of God, that ye may be able to withstand in the evil day, and having done all, to stand.

14 Stand therefore, having your loins girt about with truth, and having on the breastplate of righteousness;

15 And your feet shod with the preparation of the gospel of peace;

16 Above all, taking the shield of faith, wherewith ye shall be able to quench all the fiery darts of the wicked.

17 And take the helmet of salvation, and the sword of the Spirit, which is the word of God

Psalm 91:1-13

1 He that dwelleth in the secret place of the most High shall abide under the shadow of the Almighty.

2 I will say of the LORD, He is my refuge and my fortress: my God; in him will I trust.

3 Surely he shall deliver thee from the snare of the fowler, and from the noisome pestilence.

4 He shall cover thee with his feathers, and under his wings shalt thou trust: his truth shall be thy shield and buckler.

5 Thou shalt not be afraid for the terror by night; nor for the arrow that flieth by day;

6 Nor for the pestilence that walketh in darkness; nor for the destruction that wasteth at noonday.

7 A thousand shall fall at thy side, and ten thousand at thy right hand; but it shall not come nigh thee.

8 Only with thine eyes shalt thou behold and see the reward of the wicked.

9Because thou hast made the LORD, which is my refuge, even the most High, thy habitation;

10 There shall no evil befall thee, neither shall any plague come nigh thy dwelling.

11 For he shall give his angels charge over thee, to keep thee in all thy ways.

12 They shall bear thee up in their hands, lest thou dash thy foot against a stone.

13 Thou shalt tread upon the lion and adder: the young lion and the dragon shalt thou trample under feet.

Deuteronomy 28:1-14

1 And it shall come to pass, if thou shalt hearken diligently unto the voice of the LORD thy God, to observe and to do all his commandments which I command thee this day, that the LORD thy God will set thee on high above all nations of the earth:

2 And all these blessings shall come on thee, and overtake thee, if thou shalt hearken unto the voice of the LORD thy God.

3 Blessed shalt thou be in the city, and blessed shalt thou be in the field.

4 Blessed shall be the fruit of thy body, and the fruit of thy ground, and the fruit of thy cattle, the increase of thy kine, and the flocks of thy sheep.

5 Blessed shall be thy basket and thy store.

6 Blessed shalt thou be when thou comest in, and blessed shalt thou be when thou goest out.

7 The LORD shall cause thine enemies that rise up against thee to be smitten before thy face: they shall come out

against thee one way, and flee before thee seven ways.

8 The LORD shall command the blessing upon thee in thy storehouses, and in all that thou settest thine hand unto; and he shall bless thee in the land which the LORD thy God giveth thee.

9 The LORD shall establish thee an holy people unto himself, as he hath sworn unto thee, if thou shalt keep the commandments of the LORD thy God, and walk in his ways.

10 And all people of the earth shall see that thou art called by the name of the LORD; and they shall be afraid of thee.

11 And the LORD shall make thee plenteous in goods, in the fruit of thy body, and in the fruit of thy cattle, and in the fruit of thy ground, in the land which the LORD sware unto thy fathers to give thee.

12 The LORD shall open unto thee his good treasure, the heaven to give the rain unto thy land in his season, and to bless all the work of thine hand: and thou shalt lend unto many nations, and

thou shalt not borrow.

13 And the LORD shall make thee the head, and not the tail; and thou shalt be above only, and thou shalt not be beneath; if that thou hearken unto the commandments of the LORD thy God, which I command thee this day, to observe and to do them:

14 And thou shalt not go aside from any of the words which I command thee this day, to the right hand, or to the left, to go after other gods to serve them.

Let the Wind Blow

Introduction

In the beginning God created the heaven and the earth. And the earth was without form, and void; and darkness was upon the face of the deep. And the Spirit of God moved upon the face of the waters. Gen 1:1-2 KJV

Here in the opening verses of the Bible, we see our first reference to the Holy Spirit. The Hebrew word translated Spirit, 'ru-ach' literally means wind or breath. God exhaled and His holy breath blew as a creative wind across the landscape of the universe. The word translated move, 'ra-chaph' means to hover or flutter. From this descriptive wording we gain insight into Matthew's narrative of Jesus' baptism:

And Jesus, when he was baptized, went up straightway out of the water: and, lo, the heavens were opened unto him, and he saw the Spirit of God descending like a dove, and lighting upon him ... Matt

3:16 KJV

The picture of the Holy Spirit hovering or fluttering like a dove is significant. Just as in Genesis one, we see Him move as the Word speaks. Jesus, the Son of God, the Incarnate Word, was the central agent of creation in Genesis chapter one. The Father willed it, the Word spoke it, and the Spirit moved eventually culminating in the creation of Adam, the first man:

In the beginning was the Word, and the Word was with God, and the Word was God. The same was in the beginning with God. All things were made by him; and without him was not anything made that was made ... And the Word was made flesh, and dwelt among us ...John1:1-3;8

Now, as we read in Matthew three, Jesus is about to launch His earthly ministry, and the creative power of the Holy Spirit is once again overshadowing the proceedings and announcing the revelation of a new type of man, the second Adam.

The first man Adam was made a living soul; the last Adam was made a quickening spirit ...The first man is of the earth, earthy: the second man is the Lord from heaven. 2 Cor 15:45;47

The New Testament word translated Spirit (and sometimes wind) is 'pneuma'. This is the Greek equivalent of the Hebrew 'ru-ach'. Both denote a wind, a breath, or a blowing. In Jewish usage they both also had an enlarged definition which included the concept of spirit. This, no doubt, had its origin in the Genesis account of man's creation:

*And the LORD God formed man of the dust of the ground, and breathed into his nostrils the **breath of life**; and man became a living soul. Gen 2:7 KJV (emphasis mine)*

While the Hebrew word used in Genesis 2 is 'nesh-aw-mah' the word 'ru-ach' is used interchangeably as a synonym within the book of Genesis:

*And, behold, I, even I, do bring a flood of waters upon the earth, to destroy all flesh, wherein is the **breath of life** (ru-ach), from under heaven; and every thing that is in the earth shall die. Genesis 6:17 (emphasis mine)*

Just as we see the 'ru-ach' wind moving on the newly created earth in Genesis chapter one; we also see Him at work in the reshaping of the world after the flood:

*And God remembered Noah, and every living thing, and all the cattle that was with him in the ark: and God made a **wind** to pass over the earth, and the waters asswaged; The fountains also of the deep and the windows of heaven were stopped, and the rain from heaven* *was restrained; And the waters returned from off the earth continually: and after the end of the hundred and fifty days the waters were abated. Gen 8:2-3 KJV (emphasis mine)*

While the verses I have quoted so far are all interrelated, I don't want to focus only on those type of verses. I merely wished to lay a foundation on which to build. My purpose is to show that the work of God's breath or wind is not limited to the acts of creation or re-creation. It is involved in many aspects of God's relationship with us. Throughout the scripture there are references to this Holy wind manifesting Itself in human affairs, especially with the nation and people of Israel. This is a facet of God's interaction with His people that often is missed due to the many words used in translation to describe it ...wind, breath, spirit; God spoke and the Spirit moved, or as scripture relates it many times; the wind blew. The wind was a physical manifestation of the move of the Spirit.

In fact, Jesus himself used the **physical wind** as an example of the moving of the Spirit:

Marvel not that I said unto thee, Ye must be born again. The wind bloweth where it listeth, and thou hearest the sound thereof, but canst not tell whence it cometh, and whither it goeth: so is every one that is born of the Spirit. John 3:8

His reference to the elusiveness of the wind in describing the Spirit is the main reason for this book. I will attempt to focus on this aspect of God's nature and character and bring to this subject a measure of clarity in hopes that you will begin to say with me: let the wind blow!

Judgment

The earliest incident of God intervening in the affairs of the nation of Israel via His holy wind is found in Exodus chapter 10:

And Moses and Aaron came in unto Pharaoh, and said unto him, Thus saith the LORD God of the Hebrews, How long wilt thou refuse to humble thyself before me? let my people go, that they may serve me. Else, if thou refuse to let my people go, behold, to morrow will I bring the locusts into thy coast: And they shall cover the face of the earth, that one cannot be able to see the earth: and they shall eat the residue of that which is escaped, which remaineth unto you from the hail, and shall eat every tree which groweth for you out of the field: And Moses stretched forth his rod over the land of Egypt, ...and the LORD brought an east wind upon the land all that day, and all that night; and when it was morning, the east wind brought the locusts. And the locusts went up over all the land of Egypt, and rested in all the coasts of Egypt: very grievous were they ... And the LORD turned a mighty strong west wind, which took away the locusts, and cast them into the Red sea; there remained not one locust in all the coasts of Egypt. Ex 10:3-5;13-14;19

Here we see God moving in judgment against the Egyptians for oppressing His chosen people. When Pharaoh refused to obey God's command, delivered by Moses, to let the Israelites leave Egypt, the east wind blew in a devastating swarm of locusts which devoured everything in its path. This is an example of the wind of God moving in a situation in a miraculous way. Only when Pharaoh relents does an west wind come and blow them away.

We also see God speaking judgment against the nation of Israel itself and using terms relating to His supernatural wind:

Because my people hath forgotten me, they have burned incense to vanity, and they have caused them to stumble in their ways from the ancient paths, to walk in paths, in a way not cast up; To make their land desolate, and a perpetual hissing; every one that passeth thereby shall be astonished, and wag his head. I will scatter them as with an **east wind** *before the enemy; I will shew them the back, and not the face, in the day of their calamity. Jeremiah18:15-17 (emphasis mine)*

Thy mother is like a vine in thy blood, planted by the waters: she was fruitful and full of branches by reason of many waters. And she had strong rods for the sceptres of them that bare rule, and her stature was exalted among the thick *branches, and she appeared in her height with the multitude of her branches. But she was plucked up in fury, she was cast down to the ground, and the **east wind** dried up her fruit: her strong rods were broken and withered; the fire consumed them. And now she is planted in the wilderness, in a dry and thirsty ground. And fire is gone out of a rod of her branches, which hath devoured her fruit, so that she hath no strong rod to be a sceptre to rule. This is a lamentation, and shall be for a lamentation. Ezek 19:11-14 (emphasis mine)*

The phrase east wind, 'qadim ruach' in Hebrew, is virtually always associated with God's judgment; whether against Israel or in vengeance against her enemies. God will judge His people, and will **always** judge those who oppress His chosen ones.

And if the righteous scarcely be saved, where shall the ungodly and the sinner appear? 1 Peter 4:18

*The ungodly are not so: but are like the chaff which the **wind** driveth away. Therefore the ungodly shall not stand in the judgment, nor sinners in the congregation of the righteous. For the LORD knoweth the way of the righteous: but the way of the ungodly shall perish. Psalms 1:5-6 (emphasis mine)*

Notice that once again the wind is used as a symbolic description of the judgment to come on God's enemies. Jesus uses the same symbols to describe the fate of two people; the 'wise man' and the 'foolish man':

Therefore whosoever heareth these sayings of mine, and doeth them, I will liken him unto a wise man, which built his house upon a rock: And the rain descended, and the floods came, and the winds blew, and beat upon that house; and it fell not: for it was founded upon a rock. And every one that heareth these sayings of mine, and doeth them not, shall be likened unto a foolish man, which built his house upon the sand: And the rain descended, and the floods came, and the winds blew, and beat upon that house; and it fell: and great was the fall of it. Matt 7:24-27

In our lives we will face what the scripture calls 'trials' and 'tests'. Just as the wind blew on each of these individuals' houses testing them, we are going to be tested. When we are, we must rely on God for strength to pass the test or trial. What part of your life is being tested right now?

Protection

One of the least recognized forms of God's holy wind is the whirlwind. This is more often than not because the wording is far different than in the cases of just the wind blowing. We see this manifestation in many instances; however, I want to concentrate on one in particular. This is a case of protection being given to God's people.

And the angel of God, which went before the camp of Israel, removed and went behind them; and the pillar of the cloud went from before their face, and stood behind them: And it came between the camp of the Egyptians and the camp of Israel; and it was a cloud and darkness to them, but it gave light by night to these: so that the one came not near the other all the night. Exodus 14:19-20

The Hebrew word for pillar is ah-mud, and simply means an upright column.

The word translated cloud is the Hebrew word aw-nawn, and is used specifically of what is called by theologians the 'Theophanic' cloud or glory cloud. This is a cloud that is seen throughout the Old Testament as an appearance of the manifest presence of the Almighty. We first see the 'pillar of cloud' in Exodus chapter 13:

And the LORD went before them by day in a pillar of a cloud, to lead them the way; and by night in a pillar of fire, to give them light; to go by day and night: He took not away the pillar of the cloud by day, nor the pillar of fire by night, from before the people. Ex 13:21-22

While **this particular** description doesn't directly reference wind, others similar scriptures do. Ezekiel describes his vision of the glory of God this way:

Now it came to pass in the thirtieth year, in the fourth month, in the fifth day of the month, as I was among the captives by the river of Chebar, that the heavens were opened, and I saw visions of God. And I looked, and, behold, a whirlwind came out of the north, a great cloud, and a fire infolding itself, and a brightness was about it, and out of the midst thereof as the colour of amber, out of the midst of the fire. Ezekiel 1:1;4

The Living Bible renders it this way:

I saw, in this vision, a great storm coming toward me from the north, driving before it a huge cloud glowing with fire, with a mass of fire inside that flashed continually ...

Notice the description of the cloud as a whirlwind or a great storm. Both are related to **wind.** In fact, the Hebrew words translated 'whirlwind' are ru-ach ca-ar; ru-ach meaning wind and ca-ar meaning a storm or tempest (often translated by itself as 'whirlwind') Notice also that Ezekiel's description includes fire in the storm or whirlwind. Both passages describe clouds with fire and result in wind or a whirlwind. I believe this leaves us on firm footing to understand Moses' pillar of cloud as a whirlwind with fire just like Ezekiel's.

In 2 Kings chapter 2 we see Elijah taken up into heaven:

And it came to pass, when the LORD would take up Elijah into heaven by a whirlwind ... there appeared a chariot of fire, and horses of fire, and parted them both asunder; and Elijah went up by a whirlwind into heaven. 2Kings 2:1-11

Once again we have a description that includes a whirlwind and fire as a manifestation of God's presence and glory.

Now let's re-examine the passage from Exodus 14:

And it came between the camp of the Egyptians and the camp of Israel ... so that the one came not near the other all the night. Exodus 14:20

Notice that the pillar was a protection to the Israelites; not allowing the Egyptians to approach them. This separation was maintained until God allowed the Egyptians to pursue the Israelites to their own ultimate destruction.

And it came to pass, that in the morning watch the LORD looked unto the host of the Egyptians through the pillar of fire and of the cloud, and troubled the host of the Egyptians ...Exodus 14:24

The phrase 'looked unto' literally means 'looked down upon'. Notice that He is looking through the pillar of fire and cloud. I believe He looked down and sent His wind to trouble them and to close the sea over them completing their destruction.

The Lord never promised us that no enemies would rise against us; only that He would protect us from them. What enemy do you need God to protect you from? Disease? Poverty? Spiritual oppression? Or maybe that enemy is yourself and your poor life choices!

Deliverance

Another arena of intervention in the lives of God's people by His holy wind is in the area of deliverance. As I noted in the last chapter, in Exodus chapter 14 we see the wind blow deliverance to Israel and destruction to the army of Egypt.

And the angel of God, which went before the camp of Israel, removed and went behind them; and the pillar of the cloud went from before their face, and stood behind them: And it came between the camp of the Egyptians and the camp of Israel; and it was a cloud and darkness to them, but it gave light by night to these: so that the one came not near the other all the night. And Moses stretched out his hand over the sea; and the LORD caused the sea to go back by a strong east wind all that night, and made the sea dry land, and the waters were a wall unto them on their right hand, and on their left. And the

Egyptians pursued, and went in after them to the midst of the sea, even all Pharaoh's horses, his chariots, and his horsemen. And it came to pass, that in the morning watch the LORD looked unto the host of the Egyptians through the pillar of fire and of the cloud, and troubled the host of the Egyptians, And took off their chariot wheels, that they drave them heavily: so that the Egyptians said, Let us flee from the face of Israel; for the LORD fighteth for them against the Egyptians. And the LORD said unto Moses, Stretch out thine hand over the sea, that the waters may come again upon the Egyptians, upon their chariots, and upon their horsemen. And Moses stretched forth his hand over the sea, and the sea returned to his strength when the morning appeared; and the Egyptians fled against it; and the LORD overthrew the Egyptians in the midst of the sea. And the waters returned, and covered the chariots, and the horsemen, and all the host of Pharaoh that came into the sea after them; there remained not so much as one of them. But the children of Israel walked upon dry land in the midst of the sea; and the waters were a wall unto them on their right hand, and on their left. Thus the LORD saved Israel that day out of the hand of the Egyptians; and Israel saw the Egyptians dead upon the sea shore. Ex 14:19-30

In the last chapter an east wind brought judgment and a west wind removed it. In this case an east wind brought deliverance to the people of Israel (but judgment to the Egyptians) by opening a highway of dry ground in the middle of the Red Sea. When the enemies of Israel, the Egyptian army, pursued them the wind was removed by God. This resulted in the entire army being drowned in the sea. The Israelites crossed into the Sinai and freedom.

God had originally sent Jacob and his sons into Egypt to preserve them during the great famine. However, they took up residence and were taken into slavery. Many times we get taken into bondage by a sin or habit in our life. God has the power to loose His holy wind into our lives and break off strongholds. What habitual sin or shortcoming do you need God's deliverance from? What devise of the enemy or baggage from your past needs to be left buried in the sea of God's forgetfulness?

Provision

Another area of movement by God's holy wind is in the area of provision. We see this in Numbers chapter 11. The Israelites have been complaining about only receiving bread from God in the form of manna even though they initially thought it was wonderful. In response God gives them birds (KJV quail) to eat. How often we receive just what we need and want from the Lord only to become dissatisfied with His blessings of provision because it doesn't fit with our ideal of what our life and provision should be like!

Ye shall not eat one day, nor two days, nor five days, neither ten days, nor twenty days; But even a whole month, until it come out at your nostrils, and it be loathsome unto you: because that ye have despised the LORD which is among you, and have wept before him, saying,

Why came we forth out of Egypt? And Moses said, The people, among whom I am, are six hundred thousand footmen; and thou hast said, I will give them flesh, that they may eat a whole month. Shall the flocks and the herds be slain for them, to suffice them? or shall all the fish of the sea be gathered together for them, to suffice them? Num 11:19-22

*And there went forth a wind from the LORD, and brought quails from the sea, and let them fall by the camp, as it were **a day's journey on this side, and as it were a day's journey on the other side, round about the camp, and as it were two cubits high upon the face of the earth**. And the people stood up all that day, and all that night, and all the next day, and they gathered the quails: he that gathered least gathered ten homers: and they spread them all abroad for themselves round about the camp. Num 11:31-32 (emphasis mine)*

The harvest God blows into our lives is

abundant beyond belief. They quail were not just for one meal, but were enough for a whole month! Verse 32 states that he that gathered the **least** gathered 10 homers, which is the equivalent in today's measure to about 80 bushels! It would have been all the Israelites could do just to transport the birds as they journeyed.

This whole incident turned into a judgment from the Lord because of their lack of faith and grumbling. The bottom line, however, is that **it was** a provision. It also points out a principle of God's permissive nature: He sometimes allows harvests or provision to come into our life even though it is not what we need but what we want. In some cases it is only by experiencing the emptiness of 'gain without God' that He will drive us back to Himself and His perfect will.

He that is greedy of gain troubleth his own house Proverbs 15:27

Perverse disputings of men of corrupt minds, and destitute of the truth, supposing that gain is godliness: from such withdraw thyself. But godliness with contentment is great gain. 1 Timothy 6:5-6

These verses point out that when God divinely blows provision into our lives, we need to be thankful for His blessings and live in contentment with those things He supplies. What area of your life are you struggling with discontentment in?

Empowerment

The last and most important example of God's holy wind invading human affairs is found in Acts chapter 2:

*And when the day of Pentecost was fully come, they were all with one accord in one place. And suddenly there came a sound from heaven as of a rushing mighty **wind**, and it filled all the house where they were sitting. And there appeared unto them cloven tongues like as of **fire**, and it sat upon each of them. And they were all filled with the Holy Ghost, and began to speak with other tongues, as the Spirit gave them utterance. Acts 2:1-4 (emphasis mine)*

Notice that just as in the Old Testament examples, there is wind and also fire present. Jesus had instructed His disciples not to leave Jerusalem until they were empowered;

And, being assembled together with them, commanded them that they should not depart from Jerusalem, but wait for the promise of the Father, which, saith he, ye have heard of me. For John truly baptized with water; but ye shall be baptized with the Holy Ghost not many days hence. Acts 1:4-5

Jesus had told them, shortly before the ascension, that they would be endued, or literally, clothed upon with power after He was gone back to heaven.

And, behold, I send the promise of my Father upon you: but tarry ye in the city of Jerusalem, until ye be endued with power from on high. Luke 24:49

This manifestation on the day of Pentecost is the fulfillment of that promise. He had also previously told them:

And I will pray the Father, and he shall give you another Comforter, that he may abide with you for ever; Even the Spirit of truth; whom the world cannot receive, because it seeth him not, neither knoweth him: but ye know him; for he dwelleth with you, and shall be in you. But the Comforter, which is the Holy Ghost, whom the Father will send in my name, he shall teach you all things, and bring all things to your remembrance, whatsoever I have said unto you.
John 14:16-17;26

The promise of the Holy Spirit was made with the revelation that He would not come until some time after the ascension.

Nevertheless I tell you the truth; It is expedient for you that I go away: for if I go not away, the Comforter will not come unto you; but if I depart, I will send him unto you. John 16:7

This promised empowerment was not just for those disciples but for all:

Therefore being by the right hand of God exalted, and having received of the Father the promise of the Holy Ghost, he hath shed forth this, which ye now see and hear ... For the promise is unto you, and to your children, and to all that are afar off, even as many as the Lord our God shall call. Acts 2:33;39

The promise is also for 'their children' and 'all that are afar off'. This means the Gentile as well as the Jew have this promise! Notice the phrase 'afar off'. This refers to the Gentile world which was lost and separated from God. Ephesians chapter 2 speaks of this separation:

That at that time ye were without Christ, being aliens from the commonwealth of Israel, and strangers from the covenants of promise, having no hope, and without God in the world: But now in Christ Jesus ye who sometimes were far off are made nigh by the blood of Christ. Ephesians 2:12-13

Once again we see those who are 'far off' referring to the Gentile world. Galatians chapter 3 makes it even plainer:

Christ hath redeemed us from the curse of the law, being made a curse for us: for it is written, Cursed is every one that hangeth on a tree: That the blessing of Abraham might come on the Gentiles through Jesus Christ; that we might receive the promise of the Spirit through faith. Galatians 3:14

The promise of the Holy Spirit according to the preceding scriptures will: empower, teach, and guide us and bring His teachings to our remembrance. In what area of your life do you need the Holy Spirit to work, fill, and empower you? To teach you? To guide you and bring His word to memory?

Prayers

In the preceding chapters we have seen God's wind move in judgment, protection, deliverance, provision, and empowerment. The following are prayers tailored to these areas and are intended to be not a form prayer; but models off which to build as you examine these aspects of your life. Let the wind blow!

Prayer for judgment:

Father God, I come to You, praying that you will give me the insight to examine myself according to 1 Corinthians 2:14 so that I will be judged by no man. Let your Spirit search me and try me to bring to light every way I need change to conform to Your image and will.

Prayer for protection:

Heavenly Father, I believe I receive Your divine protection today as I walk in Your will and Your ways. Place the pillar of Your Presence between me and every enemy that would come against me.

Prayer for deliverance:

Father I pray according to Matthew 6:13 that You would deliver me from evil and the evil one. I claim Your promise in 1 Corinthians 10:13 that you will make a way of escape for every temptation.

Prayer for provision:

Lord I come to You seeking my daily bread according to Matthew 6:11. I claim your promises of provision and plenty and blessing on everything I set my hand to according to Deuteronomy 28.

Prayer for empowerment:

Father, I come to You seeking a fresh

filing of Your Holy Spirit. I can do nothing within myself and only by His power can I accomplish anything of value. Fill me according to your word so that I can be conformed to His image.

He caused an east wind to blow in the heaven: and by his
power he brought in the south wind.
Psalms 78:21-27

The Gardener's Clothes

Introduction

There are passages in scripture that contain a slightly odd statement or phrase. We pass over them, pause, raise an eyebrow, and then read on. We very seldom, however, stop and dig into that odd turn of a word that caught our eye. The following is one such passage:

But Mary stood without at the sepulchre weeping: and as she wept, she stooped down, and looked into the sepulchre, And seeth two angels in white sitting, the one at the head, and the other at the feet, where the body of Jesus had lain. And they say unto her, Woman, why weepest thou? She saith unto them, Because they have taken away my Lord, and I know not where they have laid him. And when she had thus said, she turned herself back, and saw Jesus standing, and knew not that it was Jesus. Jesus saith unto her, Woman, why weepest thou? whom seekest thou? She, supposing him to be the gardener, saith unto him, Sir, if thou have borne him hence, tell me where thou hast laid him, and I will take him away. Jesus saith unto her, Mary. She turned herself, and saith unto him, Rabboni; which is to say, Master. John 20:11-16

The question that begs to be answered is: why did Mary think he was the gardener? There had been no mention of a gardener before and none was mentioned afterward. There must have been something that led Mary's mind in that direction. What was it? Why in her state of disconsolate grief did her mind jump to that conclusion? What made her even think along those lines in the first place?

This book is a study into those questions, their answers, and the implications for us as believers. It is a verbal archaeological dig for the gardener's clothes.

In the Beginning

The book of Genesis lays out God's creative process for us. First the heavens and the earth, followed by the refinement of them. Next the creation of all the flora and fauna; culminating in the creation of the first man: Adam. Chapter 1 gives an overview of this event:

And God said, Let us make man in our image, after our likeness: and let them have dominion over the fish of the sea, and over the fowl of the air, and over the cattle, and over all the earth, and over every creeping thing that creepeth upon the earth. So God created man in his own image, in the image of God created he him; male and female created he them. And God blessed them, and God said unto them, Be fruitful, and multiply, and replenish the earth, and subdue it: and have dominion over the fish of the sea, and over the fowl of the air, and over every living thing that moveth upon the earth. Gen 1:26-28

It is obvious from this narrative that man is to be God's agent in the earth, exercising dominion as the Lord's ambassador to his creation. He and his offspring are to fill the earth and bring it into subjection to God's will as revealed to Adam, and to produce order.

Next we see in chapter 2 a more detailed expression of these events. Adam was to be formed from the earth he was tasked with ruling:

These are the generations of the heavens and of the earth when they were created, in the day that the LORD God made the earth and the heavens, And every plant of the field before it was in the earth, and every herb of the field before it grew: for the LORD God had not caused it to rain upon the earth, and there was not a man to till the ground. But there went up a mist from the earth, and watered the whole face of the ground. And the LORD God formed man of the dust of the ground, and breathed into his nostrils the breath of life; and man became a living soul. Genesis 2:4-7

Notice the breath of life (Hebrew neshamah or spirit) being placed within Adam. This distinguished him from all the other creatures God had made before him. We then see a recounting of Adam beginning his assignment as God's steward followed by the poignant statement that there was no helper suitable for him.

... for Adam there was not found an help meet for him. And the LORD God caused a deep sleep to fall upon Adam, and he slept: and he took one of his ribs, and closed up the flesh instead thereof; And the rib, which the LORD God had taken from man, made he a woman, and brought her unto the man. And Adam said, This is now bone of my bones, and flesh of my flesh: she shall be called

Woman, because she was taken out of Man. Therefore shall a man leave his father and his mother, and shall cleave unto his wife: and they shall be one flesh. Gen 2:21-24

Adam now is fully and thoroughly equipped to carry out his life's mission. He is in a perfect environment with a perfect partner and helper. He has only to carry out his divine mandate. Sadly this situation did not last long...

The Garden and the Gardener

One other important aspect of Adam's equipping is found in Genesis 1:28. As we previously saw in this verse, Adam was given the authority to rule as God's agent in the earth.

And God blessed them, and God said unto them, Be fruitful, and multiply, and replenish the earth, and subdue it: and have dominion over the fish of the sea, and over the fowl of the air, and over every living thing that moveth upon the earth. And God said, Behold, I have given you every herb bearing seed, which is upon the face of all the earth, and every tree, in the which is the fruit of a tree yielding seed; to you it shall be for meat. Gen 1:28-29

Notice the word 'replenish'. This word in Hebrew is 'male', which means to fill. Adam and Eve were not intended to do this job alone, but their offspring were to spread out from their home base and fill the earth; subduing every part of it. In the following passages we will see Adam begin this new assignment as the Lord places him in what is to be mankind's headquarters.

And the LORD God planted a garden eastward in Eden; and there he put the man whom he had formed. And out of the ground made the LORD God to grow every tree that is pleasant to the sight, and good for food; the tree of life also in the midst of the garden, and the tree of knowledge of good and evil. Gen 2:8-9

Notice that there is no mention of a prohibition on eating of the tree of knowledge at this point. It is only after Adam is placed in the garden and given his initial instructions that the warning is given to him.

And the LORD God took the man, and put him into the garden of Eden to dress it and to keep it. And the LORD God commanded the man, saying, Of every tree of the garden thou mayest freely eat: But of the tree of the knowledge of good and evil, thou shalt not eat of it: for in the day that thou eatest thereof thou shalt surely die. Gen 2:15-17

Particularly notice the wording of verse 15: 'dress it' and 'keep it'. The word for dress in this verse is 'abad' which can mean work or labor, but also in over 80 percent of all uses in scripture is rendered 'serve'. Adam was the world's first servant leader! The word for 'keep' is 'shamar' and means to have charge over and oversee; but also carries a connotation of watching and guarding. I believe it is incredibly significant that immediately following this instruction that Adam is given the world's first rule: don't eat of the tree of knowledge. Obviously, God in his foreknowledge knew the serpent was coming and was preparing Adam to be on guard for it. God proceeds to make Eve so that Adam has a suitable helper to not only fill the earth, but to carry on the work of service in the garden.

And the LORD God caused a deep sleep to fall upon Adam, and he slept: and he took one of his ribs, and closed up the flesh instead thereof; And the rib, which the LORD God had taken from man, made he a woman, and brought her unto the man. And Adam said, This is now bone of my bones, and flesh of my flesh: she shall be called Woman, because she was taken out of Man. Therefore shall a man leave his father and his mother, and shall cleave unto his wife: and they shall be one flesh. And they were both naked, the man and his wife, and were not ashamed. Gen 2:22-25

Verse 25 of chapter 2 tells us that Adam and Eve were naked but were not ashamed. The reason for this is the fact that while they were naked physically, they were not naked spiritually. In their un-fallen state they were covered by the glory of God. Their bodies were uncovered but the spiritual condition always supersedes the physical.

The Fall

In Genesis 3 we see the single rule God gave to man undergo a testing by Satan (the serpent).

Now the serpent was more subtil than any beast of the field which the LORD God had made. And he said unto the woman, Yea, hath God said, Ye shall not eat of every tree of the garden? And the woman said unto the serpent, We may eat of the fruit of the trees of the garden: But of the fruit of the tree which is in the midst of the garden, God hath said, Ye shall not eat of it, neither shall ye touch it, lest ye die. And the serpent said unto the woman, Ye shall not surely die: For God doth know that in the day ye eat thereof, then your eyes shall be opened, and ye shall be as gods, knowing good and evil. Gen 3:1-5

There are several interesting points to be made concerning these verses. First,

Satan didn't openly contradict God's edict; he simply called it into question, planting the seeds of doubt. The effects of this become obvious by Eve's response. She inaccurately conveys God's words by adding 'neither touch it'; a phrase we have no record in scripture of the Lord ever saying. The serpent then moves in for the kill by promising hidden knowledge; i.e. implying God is holding out on Adam and Eve.

Here was Eve's reaction:

And when the woman saw that the tree was good for food, and that it was pleasant to the eyes, and a tree to be desired to make one wise, she took of the fruit thereof, and did eat, and gave also unto her husband with her; and he did eat. And the eyes of them both were opened, and they knew that they were naked; and they sewed fig leaves together, and made themselves aprons. And they heard the voice of the LORD God walking in the garden in the cool of the day: and Adam and his wife hid themselves from the presence of the LORD God amongst the trees of the garden. Gen 3:6-8

Here she succumbs to the three types of temptation recorded by 1 John 2:16: the lust of the flesh (good to eat), the lust of the eyes (pleasant to the eye), and the pride of life (desired to make one wise). Eve looked over the tree, weighed the consequences as she saw them, and fell for all three. Not only did she eat of the fruit of the tree, she gave some to Adam (who was standing there with her!) and he followed her lead.

They recognized immediately that they were naked and attempted to remedy the situation. Like all fallen humans they addressed the symptom of nakedness rather than the disease of sin. Their condition hadn't changed physically, but their spiritual condition had changed resulting in their recognition of a physical condition that already existed.

When they sinned, their eyes were opened to their physical condition because their spiritual condition had changed which in turn changed their viewpoint of the events and perception of themselves and their surroundings: again the spiritual always supersedes the physical. They proceeded to makes 'aprons' out of fig leaves. Fig leaves are singularly itchy and irritating to human skin; an apt symbol of the unsustainable and untenable nature of human efforts to cover their sinfulness. The Hebrew word translated here as 'apron' refers to a loin-cloth type garment. This measure would have covered their human nakedness but it didn't cover their hearts where the root problem lay.

The Wrong Tree

Adam, who had been given permission to eat of every tree except the tree of knowledge, including the tree of life, chose the wrong tree. This had disastrous consequences not only for himself, but for all his offspring. God in his infinite mercy evicted them from the garden to prevent them from eating from the tree of life and living eternally in their fallen condition.

And the eyes of them both were opened, and they knew that they were naked; and they sewed fig leaves together, and made themselves aprons. And they heard the voice of the LORD God walking in the garden in the cool of the day: and Adam and his wife hid themselves from the presence of the LORD God amongst the trees of the garden. Gen 3:7-8

When he sinned his eyes were opened

to his fallen human condition but were simultaneously closed to the spiritual realm. Adam by sinning had lost his 'gardeners clothes' and all that they comprised. Man lost his glory covering and so now recognized his nakedness. He innately knew the aprons were insufficient, as evidenced by the fact that he hid from his creator. .

And the LORD God called unto Adam, and said unto him, Where art thou? And he said, I heard thy voice in the garden, and I was afraid, because I was naked; and I hid myself. Gen 3:9-10

Notice also that although he and Eve 'heard the voice of the Lord'; they didn't see him. They only heard. The processes of spiritual death and separation from God were already working in them. Adam also lost his dominion and now recognized his helplessness. He is evicted from his home and sent out to face a far less hospitable environment than he was used to. Without his gardener's clothes he was left to fend for himself in a world in which he had no power or authority. The curses of Genesis 3 told him plainly that the ground would be adverse to his efforts.

Finally, he lost his spirit life and recognized his sinfulness. This causes Adam and Eve to do the most incomprehensible, yet thoroughly human act in this narrative. They rush headlong into the very source of their problems. They climbed up into the tree! The Hebrew word in Genesis 3:8 is singular. This means the rendering should actually be 'they hid themselves in the midst of the tree.' How typical of the reaction fallen humanity has to the shame of sin; they tend to plunge right into the middle of what is actually destroying them!

Needing a New Set of Clothes

Just as Adam and Eve realized that their current mode of dress was insufficient to cover their nakedness (sinfulness) before Almighty God, the Lord too recognized this need and made a 'down payment' on the new set of clothes he had in mind for fallen mankind. In Genesis 3: 21 is this simple statement:

Unto Adam also and to his wife did the LORD God make coats of skins, and clothed them. Gen 3:21

It is essential to note that these are coats not aprons. The Hebrew word here is 'kethoneth', which refers to a long shirt-like tunic. It covered all of them. This was the first step in a long history of God's plan for man's redemption. Isaiah portrays a prophetic description of the new clothes that God was preparing for mankind:

I will greatly rejoice in the LORD, my soul shall be joyful in my God; for he hath clothed me with the garments of salvation, he hath covered me with the robe of righteousness, as a bridegroom decketh himself with ornaments, and as a bride adorneth herself with her jewels.
Isaiah 61:10

This passage was a revelation of what the Lord was doing in this arena. It said to the nation of Israel that what he had provided in Genesis 3 was only temporary and that something better, much better, was coming.

What Adam had done had to be undone. The gardener's clothes had to someway, someday be restored. Isaiah is giving us a glimpse at what this new set of clothes would look like and what they would encompass.

The Apostle Paul gives us a New Testament insight into this situation as well. He penned these words in 2

Corinthians 5:

For we know that if our earthly house of this tabernacle were dissolved, we have a building of God, an house not made with hands, eternal in the heavens. For in this we groan, earnestly desiring to be clothed upon with our house which is from heaven: If so be that being clothed we shall not be found naked. For we that are in this tabernacle do groan, being burdened: not for that we would be unclothed, but clothed upon, that mortality might be swallowed up of life. 2 Cor 5:1-4

Here we see once again that the essential clothing in question is not material, but spiritual. It also describes the inner turmoil of our fallen human spirits wanting to be clothed with the new and better suit! (more about this in the final chapter)

The Second Adam

Adam rebelled against God and committed high treason by forfeiting control of the earth to Satan. If what he had done was to be undone; there had to be a second Adam. Adam was the first member and the progenitor of a whole race of fallen humans. For his act to be righted there had to be another Adam that was the firstborn of another, new, and better race. In 1 Corinthians 15 Paul gives a lengthy discourse on the resurrection, the spiritual body, and the rapture. He includes this statement:

And so it is written, The first man Adam was made a living soul; the last Adam was made a quickening spirit. Howbeit that was not first which is spiritual, but that which is natural; and afterward that which is spiritual. The first man is of the earth, earthy: the second man is the Lord from heaven. 1 Cor 15:45-47

Here 'the first Adam', the Adam of the Genesis account, is described as a living soul. The 'last Adam', referring to Christ, is a quickening or life-giving spirit. Paul then reiterates the principle that the spiritual takes pre-eminence over the physical. He then makes a pointed statement that the first man (Adam) was earthy; the second man (Christ) was the Lord from heaven. We see clearly the mortality of Adam after the fall. The word translated 'earthy' here denotes soil/earth that is dug or piled up. This is a symbolic and prophetic picture of Adam's nature and origin as Genesis says God formed him from the dust of the earth. It also speaks of the fact that Adam was God's gardener; a cultivator of the ground. The immediate problem Adam faced, however, was the hostile environment and soil. Man can still cultivate the earth but it is difficult. The earth is under the curse of sin the same as its erstwhile masters. The fact is, the curses of Genesis 3 were not placed on man by God. They were self-inflicted by the act of sinful rebellion. A look at the Hebrew words used in Genesis 3 confirm this: all are passive voice indicating that God was not the agent of their activation; he was merely pronouncing what was already happening in the spiritual realm. Creation was degraded under the curse of sin, and even now continues that process, as a result of the fall.

This verse also declares the divinity of Christ: 'the Lord from heaven'. This contrast highlights the need for the second, or last Adam to be superior to the first; both in nature and in character. Again, Paul tells us that Adam was living, but Christ was a life-giver!

Redemption

For Christ to be eligible to be mankind's redeemer he had to be both fully human and fully divine. He had to be fully human or he would have simply been God masquerading in a man suit. He had to be fully divine in order to be free from the defilement of sin that was passed down from Adam to all humankind. Along with this paradox of his dual natures there had to be one more ingredient: he had to be tested by sin just as all other humans are.

For we have not an high priest which cannot be touched with the feeling of our infirmities; but was in all points tempted like as we are, yet without sin. Heb 4:15

In the following scriptures we will see that he was not only tempted by the enemy but that the encounter was orchestrated by God!

And Jesus being full of the Holy Ghost returned from Jordan, and was led by the Spirit into the wilderness, Being forty days tempted of the devil. And in those days he did eat nothing: and when they were ended, he afterward hungered. And the devil said unto him, If thou be the Son of God, command this stone that it be made bread. And Jesus answered him, saying, It is written, That man shall not live by bread alone, but by every word of God. And the devil, taking him up into an high mountain, shewed unto him all the kingdoms of the world in a moment of time. And the devil said unto him, All this power will I give thee, and the glory of them: for that is delivered unto me; and to whomsoever I will I give it. If thou therefore wilt worship me, all shall be thine. And Jesus answered and said unto him, Get thee behind me, Satan: for it is written, Thou shalt worship the Lord thy God, and him only shalt thou serve. And he brought him to Jerusalem, and set him on a pinnacle of the temple, and said unto him, If thou be the Son of God, cast thyself down from hence: For it is written, He shall give his angels charge over thee, to keep thee: And in their hands they shall bear thee up, lest at any time thou dash thy foot against a stone. And Jesus answering said unto him, It is said, Thou shalt not tempt the Lord thy God. And when the devil had ended all the temptation, he departed from him for a season. Luke 4:1-13

Jesus had exactly the same choices, involving the same three types of temptation, as Eve: the lust of the flesh; the lust of the eye; and the pride of life. He chose at every point to resist the temptations and submit to the Father's will. Jesus rejected the tree of knowledge and chose the tree of life. The cross appears to be the tree of death, but to us it is the tree of life. Adam chose the wrong tree, the tree he should have rejected, and lost his gardener's clothes. Jesus chose the tree he didn't have to and got his gardener's clothes. Adam sinned and the effects worked from the outside (the fruit) inward resulting in spiritual death. Jesus shunned sin and the redemption it produced worked from the inside out. His spirit was crucified from before creation as he was 'the lamb slain before the foundation of the world.' His soul (mind, will, emotions) was crucified in the garden when he said 'Father not my will but thine'. His body then was crucified on the tree he could have avoided:

Thinkest thou that I cannot now pray to my Father, and he shall presently give me more than twelve legions of angels? Matt 26:53

Just as the Old Testament tabernacle was built from the inside out; redemption was authored from the inside out.

The New Suit

In light of the illumination gained in these past chapters let's reexamine Isaiah 61:

I will greatly rejoice in the LORD, my soul shall be joyful in my God; for he hath clothed me with the garments of salvation, he hath covered me with the robe of righteousness, as a bridegroom decketh himself with ornaments, and as a bride adorneth herself with her jewels. Isaiah 61:10

There are two articles of clothing listed here: the garment of salvation, and the robe of righteousness. Just as redemption was purchased by Christ from the inside out, the new suit will be manifested from the inside out. First, the garment of salvation is received when we become believers in Jesus Christ as our Lord and Saviour. This addresses the dead condition of our spirit man.

Just as Adam died spiritually when he ate that fruit, we too die spiritually when we reach the age at which we have reason and knowledge sufficient to be responsible before God for our sins. Second, we receive the robe of righteousness as we are transformed in our mind, will, and emotions into the image and likeness of the mind of Christ. This process is also called sanctification. Notice however that there is no mention of our physical bodies. Having been born, lived, and died under the Old Covenant, Isaiah had no revelation of a new body to come. This knowledge was only revealed after Christ's resurrection and ascension. The Apostle Paul began during his ministry to reveal these revelations to the church. For instance, let's revisit 1 Corinthians 15:

It is sown a natural body; it is raised a spiritual body. There is a natural body, and there is a spiritual body... and as we have borne the image of the earthy, we shall also bear the image of the heavenly. 1 Cor 15:44 & 49

This passage completes the prophetic picture Isaiah began 700 years earlier. Isaiah saw the spirit and soul; Paul saw the body as it was raised to immortality. John the Beloved draws this image together with what his readers already knew about the risen Messiah:

Behold, what manner of love the Father hath bestowed upon us, that we should be called the sons of God: therefore the world knoweth us not, because it knew him not. Beloved, now are we the sons of God, and it doth not yet appear what we shall be: but we know that, when he shall appear, we shall be like him; for we shall see him as he is. 1 John 3:1-2

It had to be incredibly exciting to the first century disciples, many of whom had seen Jesus' public ministry and post-resurrection appearances, to realize that they would have an immortal body just like Christ!

Mary and the Gardener

Some four-thousand years after Adam and Eve were evicted from their garden, a disciple named Mary stood weeping in another garden. Her Lord had been crucified and laid in a hand-hewn rock tomb in a small garden outside the walls of Jerusalem. It was what we westerners would call Sunday morning. To her it was the first day of the nightmare that her world, a world without her now dead Messiah, had become.

But Mary stood without at the sepulchre weeping: and as she wept, she stooped down, and looked into the sepulchre, And seeth two angels in white sitting, the one at the head, and the other at the feet, where the body of Jesus had lain. And they say unto her, Woman, why weepest thou? She saith unto them, Because they have taken away my Lord, and I know not where they have laid him. And when she had thus said, she turned herself back, and saw Jesus standing, and knew not that it was Jesus. Jesus saith unto her, Woman, why weepest thou? whom seekest thou? She, supposing him to be the gardener, saith unto him, Sir, if thou have borne him hence, tell me where thou hast laid him, and I will take him away. Jesus saith unto her, Mary. She turned herself, and saith unto him,... Master. John 20:11-16

How could Mary who had been with Jesus for most of his earthly ministry not recognize him? Why would she suppose this man whom she had known well was a gardener? Was he dressed as gardener would dress? More to the point, where did Jesus get the clothes he was wearing? A comparison to verses 4-7 makes this question even more inexplicable.

Peter therefore went forth, and that other disciple, and came to the sepulchre.4 So they ran both together: and the other disciple did outrun Peter, and came first to the sepulchre. And he stooping down, and looking in, saw the linen clothes lying; yet went he not in. Then cometh Simon Peter following him, and went into the sepulchre, and seeth the linen clothes lie, And the napkin, that was about his head, not lying with the linen clothes, but wrapped together in a place by itself. John 20:4-7

If the grave clothes and the linen cloth used to wrap his head were in the tomb, what was he wearing? We know from John 19 that the Roman soldiers attending to his crucifixion took his clothing:

Then the soldiers, when they had crucified Jesus, took his garments, and made four parts, to every soldier a part; and also his coat: now the coat was without seam, woven from the top throughout. They said therefore among themselves, Let us not rend it, but cast lots for it, whose it shall be: that the scripture might be fulfilled, which saith,

They parted my raiment among them, and
for my vesture they did cast lots. These things therefore the soldiers did. John 19:23-24

The answer to all these questions lies at the heart of what Jesus' earthly mission was about. His ministry was one of reconciliation of creation to his Father, but his primary task was redemption. That redemption as we have seen comprises body, soul, and spirit; but it also includes all that Adam lost in the fall. When Jesus arose from the rock tomb he was wearing his gardener's clothes! That is why Mary didn't recognize him; she had never before encountered God's gardener. By his act of redemption he had regained that glory covering, i.e. the gardener's clothes that Adam had lost. Not only that but also the power and dominion that came with them.

Notice that Jesus never made any claims

about His power and authority until after the resurrection. Now he makes a most audacious statement; one that no one but the glorified Son of God himself could make:

And Jesus came and spake unto them, saying, All power is given unto me in heaven and in earth. Go ye therefore, and teach all nations, baptizing them in the name of the Father, and of the Son, and of the Holy Ghost: Teaching them to observe all things whatsoever I have commanded you: and, lo, I am with you alway, even unto the end of the world. Amen. Matt 28:18-20

This is his way of staking a claim on the total authority and dominion over the creation that Adam forfeited. In the same passage he then delegates that dominion and authority to us as believers. We are the children of a new race; the redeemed. Romans 8 confirms this idea:

For whom he did foreknow, he also did predestinate to be conformed to the image of his Son, that he might be the firstborn among many brethren. Romans 8:29

Christ was the firstborn of this new race of redeemed men and women and we are his younger siblings. All that he won in his death battle with Satan has been passed down to us. We simply must operate in that dominion, power and authority:

Herein is our love made perfect, that we may have boldness in the day of judgment: because as he is, so are we in this world. 1 John 4:17